Design Thinking for Smaller Enterprise Development

Design Thinking for Smaller Enterprise Development captures the zeitgeist and concerns of the new Millennium and offers a fresh view on how business can be successful by benefiting the wider society it should serve. It also highlights the systemic negative impact of a consumption- and profit-focussed economy and introduces an original model – SOCIETALByDesign™ – as a constructive alternative to relentless resource depletion, through an agile, adaptive, and respectful enterprise, which protects nature and civilisation and embraces a balanced and holistic purpose to serve people, planet and a positive legacy, as the heart of its very reason of being. The original SOCIETALByDesign™ model positions purpose, principles, framework and current techniques for a modern business to utilise and holistically integrate benefits for employees, society and environment thought its products and services. The SOCIETALByDesign™ model links purpose and business and synthesises an operating model that can be adopted, adapted and applied by any enterprise wishing to focus on shared prosperity and the good of people and planet instead of profit at any price.

The book is intended for business practitioners such as business founders and owners, angel investors, entrepreneurs, portfolio managers of investment funds, managers and leaders of companies large and small. It is also helpful for external business and organisation development consultants, mentors, coaches and specialists who provide services and expertise to enterprises design, change and optimisation. Because the book provides a practitioner's perspective on business, it can also be useful to students, lecturers and academics.

Adina Tarry is an AI & O/D strategist, psychologist, accredited coach, Visiting Lecturer and author of *Coaching with Careers and AI in Mind*. Adina's consulting practice is informed by international business experience, psychology and cross cultural expertise, academic research, science, technology and ongoing professional development.

Design Thinking for Smaller Enterprise Development

A SOCIETALByDesign™ Model for Adaptation to a Digital Age

Adina Tarry

Routledge
Taylor & Francis Group

LONDON AND NEW YORK

First published 2020
by Routledge
2 Park Square, Milton Park, Abingdon, Oxon OX14 4RN

and by Routledge
52 Vanderbilt Avenue, New York, NY 10017

Routledge is an imprint of the Taylor & Francis Group, an informa business

British Library Cataloguing-in-Publication Data
A catalogue record for this book is available from the British Library

Library of Congress Cataloging-in-Publication Data
A catalog record for this book has been requested

ISBN: 978-0-367-26440-6 (hbk)
ISBN: 978-0-429-29325-2 (ebk)

Typeset in Baskerville
by Apex CoVantage, LLC

This book is dedicated to all the large and small organisations which have offered me, during an international career, a safe and exciting environment where I could use and develop my talent, be rewarded for my contribution and grow amongst people who supported, mentored and inspired me to become a better professional version of myself.

To all my memorable colleagues and managers who have naturally extended their gift for collaboration and vision, to enable me and our teams to be at our best. They have also been curious and respectful enough to learn from us, as much as we have valued and enjoyed learning from them.

Contents

Acknowledgements

My special thanks to Michael Arthur for patiently listening, lightening the mood with an inimitable brand of humour and offering a uniquely "contrary" constructive perspective, all of which helped me streamline arguments, reshape contents and realise my vision for this book.

About the author

Adina Tarry (born Adina Mironovici) is an AI & Enterprise optimisation strategist, business psychologist, professional accredited executive, business and career coach, visiting lecturer and speaker. Her professional practice is informed by science and technology, extensive international business experience, applied business psychology, cross-cultural savvy and a lifelong dedication to continued learning. Adina uses divergent thinking, an integrated multidisciplinary and a cross-functional body of knowledge and experience to embrace a solution-focussed approach in enterprise design and development, to enable enterprises to adapt to change and successfully transition into the world of the fourth digital revolution and its wide impact on people, business and society. Her overarching thinking model draws from dialectics and complexity thinking, applied agile and design processes used to develop the complex businesses of the future that need to refocus purpose and objectives on to people and their capacity to innovate and generate solutions in uncertain and ambiguous contexts. Adina strongly advocates enterprise design and development that enables people to be at their best and in so doing create an environment that nurtures the most effective and valuable enterprise capability of all: the endless curiosity, resilience, creativity and innovation that results from a motivated, engaged and purposely focussed human ingenuity, in the service of individuals, business, society and a sustainable technology-enabled humanistic civilisation.

Introduction

In 2018, I published the book *Coaching with Careers and AI in Mind*, focussing on career management and personal development fit for our digital age and how technology affects individual life and work at the dawn of the fourth digital revolution. But as I was writing that book, I realised that a lot was still left to be said to cover the other side of the world of work, namely the small and medium businesses and enterprises of all sizes, where integrated knowledge and practice provide the wider context for people to unfold their working lives.

I decided to create a complement to my book on careers by shifting the focus from individual work to groups and teams set in the organisational and technological context of our age to explore the fascinating, complex and dynamic world of business. Reflecting the essence of our current wider challenges and questions, this perspective places people at the centre of business and society, demonstrating how the success and happiness of our own working lives and professional fulfilment feeds back to help individuals, enterprises and society at large to contemplate an uncertain digital horizon with a better chance to act with competence towards realising the optimistic version of the future.

To this end, I used the experience of my own decades of professional life, in which I have spent a lot of time learning about and delivering my contribution but equally examining how my career and life have panned out and what have been the major influences to this particular professional history in terms of inputs and outcomes. Following my two successive careers, one in business delivery and a second in management consulting, I gained the sense that through this modern Scientist-Practitioner approach to knowledge and experience, backed by a dedicate and diverse continued personal and professional development activity, I have eventually accumulated sufficient knowledge and reflective findings to be able to share it in different ways, including writing this book.

Embracing a polymath capability

The first main influence in the way my mind was going to develop later was my early exposure and great fascination with science fiction.

Unlike most children, I was raised on short sci-fi stories and completely bypassed fairy tales to the point that to this day, I am not familiar with many related references that a regular six-year-old may have. But there is a fundamental difference in the way my mind was wired because of this unusual exposure. Instead of having visions of grannies who are in fact wolves lying in wait to devour little children, or helpless and bewitched innocent boys and girls lost in the dark and traitorous forests full of slithering evil, wandering aimlessly and hoping to be rescued by good fairies and valiant princes, and all the terrifying plots of threat and mortal danger that frankly disturb me even as an adult, I developed a vision and enjoyment of a different kind.

My imagined world was filled with pictures of endless universes and mysterious horizons, brought to life by the quest for discovery and confidence in possibilities of highly capable men and women who together overcame adversity and pursued their curiosity and ambition to push the boundaries of knowledge and go where no one has treaded before. I have been always looking for that first small human step that represented a giant leap for humankind. Despite numerous and unexpected challenges, the essence of these messages was that hope, curiosity, possibilities and achievement will triumph in light of human ingenuity.

The second influence was that of very early exposure to fine arts and being introduced to art galleries and the theory of art, well before I formally engaged with art at school.

The third influence somewhat later and more grounded in everyday life came from both my parents, who worked in international affairs and global trade. They really enjoyed their work and spoke about it with articulation and passion, which eventually triggered in me a curiosity for macro- and socioeconomics and business on a global scale.

Individually, my father was my arts and science mentor, whilst my mother was a formidable role model for project management, pragmatism and resilience. In addition, childhood travel and life abroad, surrounded by strange languages and new cultures, also greatly stirred my curiosity and accustomed me to change as soon as I could walk and talk.

This background of nature and nurture may go a long way to explain how my interests became complex and settled somewhere between individual and collective talent and achievement, between business and culture, between science and art, between detail and context, on the middle ground where such apparently opposite sides – in fact – worked together, manifesting in a synthesis, itself complex and impactful on the way life and business worked, in turn defining our own destiny.

With an MBA in international trade, I stared my first career, marked by a succession of very exciting jobs, for almost two decades working internationally for mainly blue-chip corporations but also SMEs, with the smallest having a staff of six people that included me and the largest employing some 250,000 around the globe.

This first career was long enough to enable learning and practice of almost every job except for R &D and actual engineering for which I was not qualified and included everything from sales to new product release and from international logistics and production control to manufacturing, operations, quality management, audit and financial, and human resource management, through to program and project management. I have worked in the IT, telecommunications, pharmaceutical and fashion industries, and whilst they appear dissimilar, they all shared common characteristics, namely being driven by creativity; innovation; technology; high risk, high reward; and high-competition, fast-moving cultures.

New products were designed and delivered very quickly, usually to a consumer market in which competition was high and in which product design had to satisfy a combination of problem solving and provision for a real or perceived need, desire or want, but also had to appeal to buyers in appearance, ease of use and actual or psychological turn-ons.

All in all, my early experience of work and life as a young developing adult was in fact an immersion into a world which was exciting, complex, changing, multicultural, cross-functional, and multidisciplinary and driven by innovation and ambition for excellence.

Having kept a firm eye on people in business (based on my BA in psychology), I eventually navigated to my second career outside organisations into management consulting and organisation development.

I completed an MSc in business psychology and other professional training and certifications and gained competence in most aspects of people in business. The long list includes apparently unrelated domains covering neuroscience and psychiatry, human resource strategy, team dynamics, organisational culture and leadership, national cultures, organisations development and enterprise structure and functions. From a service portfolio perspective, I added facilitation, training, lecturing, coaching, writing, presenting and interacting with peers, academics and clients across the "soft" and "hard" domains of science, business and life, as my new professional capabilities.

My second career again opened an exciting complex field of work, in which many distinct disciplines and activities seamlessly came together as an integrated and fluid perspective based on cross-functional multidisciplinary domains of knowledge and practice, necessary in transformations and change that lead to adaptation and success in business and life.

Sources of information and influences

The main sources and influences that informed me in writing this book cover formal and informal, experiential and science and research-based, personal and collective sources, alongside reflective practice, as briefly listed below:

1   Formal education, professional training and continued learning

- International education (MSc, London; MBA, Paris; BA, Bucharest)
- Memberships of numerous professional associations
- Access to primary sources: conferences, seminars, lectures and presentations
- An academic experience as a visiting lecturer, with UK and European institutions
- Writing, publishing and speaking in professional circles

2   Extensive international business experience

- Working for IBM, Alcatel, Johnson & Johnson, Bristol-Myers Squibb, Jacques Vert Plc and Ranier Pty
- Roles in manufacturing, supply chain, quality, project and program management and so on

3   A wide range of complementary bodies of knowledge

- Philosophy, psychology, social sciences, neuroscience and psychiatry
- Science and technology, artificial intelligence and robotics

4   Personal attributes, interests and life experience

- International multilingual life and work: London, Paris, Bucharest, New York and Sydney with extensive additional travel

- An enduring lifelong interest in science, technology and the arts
- Practice of tai chi, chi gong, yoga and aikido
- A passion for photography, cinema, creative writing, languages and culture

All these influences and the seamless combination of my personal and professional interests together contribute to my positive view of business and the drive to look for new opportunities for change and positive transformation, supported by a strong belief in a multidisciplinary and cross-functional approach in work and life. My values are aligned to my actions, and knowledge exchange – such as this book – is also a key part of my belief in collaboration and co-creation of positive outcomes and value for all.

Intended readership and outcomes

This book is intended for business practitioners such as business founders and owners, angel investors, entrepreneurs, portfolio managers of investment funds, managers and leaders of companies large and small.

It is also for external consultants, mentors, coaches and specialists who provide services and expertise to enterprises.

Finally, the book provides a practitioner's perspective on business that can be useful to students, lecturers and academics.

The fourth digital revolution is casting ahead for us challenges and opportunities, some predictable and some hidden, and many of the ways we have done business before no longer apply. Business as usual and long-term planning are inadequate in many economic sectors, and increasingly, business methodologies respond to this reality by creating new more agile and flexible ways of refocussing organisational resources and strategies around novel ways of working and new philosophies.

"Simple and easy" won't do when faced with complex and unpredictable demands of change and adaptation". "Move fast and learn by breaking things on the way" is another mantra that has outlived its usefulness.

The digital technology combined with a world increasingly volatile, unpredictable, complex and interconnected demands of us to sharpen and enhance our individual capabilities and engage with science and technology, develop and use higher thinking capacities, solve complex problems, use effective relationships and collaboration, embrace a cross-functional multidisciplinary way of doing things, make sense of reality and define purpose in business, work and life.

This calls for a fresh view of enterprise design and development that is integrative, complex and multilayered, reflecting this new digital world of business and life, which is what the book proposes.

Contents, structure and style

The contents of the book are structured in chapters and subchapters which are self-contained and introduce a range of diverse but interconnected bodies of knowledge alongside real-life examples, which can be used in business or to stimulate thought, reflection and learning.

The holistic perspective across scientific disciplines and business functions enables specialists, generalists and polymaths to collaborate and value the diversity of available collective knowledge, a wonderful antidote to the silo mentality that often hinders and undermines business dynamics and success, as many of us know from practice.

The language used is accessible and adapted to content to satisfy a balance between theory and practice and support informed opinions, examples, anecdotes or lessons learned, by theoretical or scientific underpinnings.

The themes and subjects covered are not treated exhaustively, and there is a lot of information and literature in the public domain that provides greater detail to those who wish to pursue a more in-depth exploration of specific topics. Instead, the book presents an integrated overview of the enterprise as a live and multilayered entity, with people at its centre.

The book is structured in three chapters, that mark the progress of the main idea around the importance of design as being fir for purpose in the digital age, because of its focus on people, empathy, innovation and openness to flexible design and re-design of contemporary solutions to the perennial fundamental human needs.

The introduction to the book precedes the first chapter and presents the credentials and professional background of the author.

The first chapter introduced the wider context of the impact of technology on customers, employees, organisations and society at large. It also showcases some of the key capabilities that people in enterprises large or small must have to be successful.

The second chapter presents design thinking and organisation development methodologies as well as a multidisciplinary cross-functional body of knowledge as fundamental building blocks to envisioning and optimising enterprise activity in the age of technology.

Chapter 3 introduces the SOCIETALByDesign™ Model as a synthesised construct of a framework, principles, capability indicators, leadership and culture combined, as a necessary approach to enable adaptive development of enterprises for the digital age.

The book ends with conclusions and calls to action. But the flow of research and writing has also brought about a welcomed – even if unintended and unplanned consequence – namely the creation of my SOCIETALByDesign™ Model. The model emerged of its own accord, as a synthesis of thoughts; a practical tool for change and development of businesses and organisations, to inform thinking and practice in management, administration, research or education.

Throughout the book, the focus on people is the unifying element that carries the central message to its conclusion.

My own research for the book gave me great pleasure and the awareness that some was knowledge I already have, some was new and exciting and some was interesting but not for me to further pursue.

With a short bibliography and a lot of sources available on the Internet, the intention of the book is to stimulate individual curiosity and motivate readers to further research this or other related topics, to reflect their personal preferences and interests and not mine.

The same personalised reaction – including the magic of emergence! – is also something that I hope to enable in others, in an age when adult learning is self-directed, individual, focussed and connected to our specific interests, passions and professional practices.

1 Trepidation and anticipation at the dawn of the new millennium of integrated digital technologies

> *The conversations and unknowns today are no longer just about technology or where it is going but increasingly about how to ensure that it is used for the greater good and for all. It is about ethics, values and purpose.*
>
> Adina Tarry, *Coaching with Careers and AI in Mind*

The survival and evolution of humankind till now has been, at least in part, explained by our unique and special ability to utilise our brains and exercise curiosity, innovation, reflection, and higher cognitive and symbolic thinking and our success in living in large social groups. These combined capabilities have enabled us individually and collectively to solve the problems and challenges presented to us by our natural environment.

Science and technology have always driven the progress of humankind, and apart from the immediate positive outcomes that applied science has had on specific activities, it has also typically caused tremendous changes in the wider social and political systems.

Mass destruction and disappearance of entire peoples have been the results of technological transfers and expansion (e.g. colonising the new world of America) but also the salvation of millions of people from disease and suffering (e.g. vaccines, clean water, sanitation, use of electricity and steam power for mass production of goods).

Human evolution, industrial revolutions and the digital age

The First Industrial Revolution used water and steam power to mechanise production (1784), which in turn gave rise to changes in social structures, the growth of industry and the benefits that came with mechanised work processes and transportation. The harnessing of power and use of engines instead of horse and human muscle power completely transformed the way people lived and worked and opened their access to another way of life in different urbanised settings.

The Second Industrial Revolution used electric power to create mass production (1890). This revolution completely changed our lives in every respect as electricity found its way in to human households and businesses, enabling an easier and more enjoyable life, serving an endless range of appliances and changing entertainment and the way we experience our lives and activities in the absence of natural light. The best way to evaluate the impact of electricity on our world is to imagine for a moment what would happen if our electricity supply simply disappears. The consequences are almost unthinkable and would swiftly take us back to the Middle Ages.

The Third Industrial Revolution used electronics and information technology (IT) to automate production (1969) and increase the range of accessible consumer goods as costs of production decreased and productivity increased. The Third Industrial Revolution offered benefits to society and improvements to the quality of life of people in many ways. Transistors and microprocessors gave rise to electronics, new materials were created and space exploration and biotechnology were supported by telecommunications and computers. IT and electronics combined increased productivity and paved the way for robotics.

Today we stand on the brink of the Fourth Industrial Revolution, also known as the Digital Revolution because of the advancement of digital technologies that are becoming increasingly integrated. This revolution has been on its way for some time and is said to be like no other before because of its scale and pace. The impact of the Digital Revolution is having and will continue to have on every single aspect of our private, public and professional lives has barely started.

This revolution is blurring the lines between digital, biological and physical domains, progressively morphing and advancing towards an outcome that is yet to be clearly charted. In motion since the middle of the 20th century, this massive change is certainly unlike anything humankind has experienced before.

The decade of 1980–1990 saw a dazzling cluster of technological advancements coming together to irreversibly transform our world. In rapid succession, the fax machine replaced the telex machine and often the post, to be in turn displaced by the PC, which superseded computer mainframes in business and then expanded into the consumer market to end up in almost every house on the planet in various desktop and laptop guises. Information management became fast and flexible and reduced personal and business transactions from days and weeks to hours and seconds.

All these fast, unstoppable and significant changes led to rapid growth in connectivity and a greater complexity of exchanges. The new technologies provided opportunities for the creation of integrated software to run manufacturing, financial transactions, ordering of materials and services in the supply chain and sales and after-sales service, and they ultimately placed "everything online".

In addition, the new software generation was modular, scalable, integrated and housed in increasingly portable and miniaturised devices literally linking everything to everything and everyone, bringing together the head and tail of the most complex of business processes. This aligned all aspects of the value and supply chain, from customer demand to raw materials, logistics and distribution, after-sales support, customer satisfaction surveys, consumer behaviour and back to research and development, to restart the business cycle anew.

The analogue star performers – IT and telecommunications (Telcos) – themselves evolved and advanced to the next level because of the increased processing power of integrated circuits (also known as micro-chips), and they formed the formidable information and communications technology (ICT), a hybrid of IT and Telcos that continues to evolve today in its integrated and digital guise, supporting the future of artificial intelligence (AI) and robotics.

The Internet then opened the gates of information, products and services to all who could access a PC. At the same time, the Baby Boomer generation was disrupting monopolies by challenging established norms and business practices and being what millennials will become some thirty years later. Budget airlines open the skies to masses of enthusiastic travellers who went abroad for holidays and work. Alongside information, people, too, could move around the world in greater numbers and faster than ever before.

Today more people travel from any point to any other point on the planet faster and cheaper than ever before. Such movement of people across the planet and at such speed has never been seen before, and with the air travel monopolies broken and air travel being so affordable, there is no stopping this phenomenon of travel and migration for both tourism and economic reasons.

The digital age, an age like no other

It is the scope, velocity and systemic impact that make the Fourth Industrial Revolution unprecedented and unique. It evolves at an exponential rather than linear pace, and it is disrupting the entire old order of industry, economy and society on a global scale. The depths and breadth of the digital revolution are challenging every existing system from family-owned small businesses all the way to regulation, governance, politics and the notion of nation states.

The Fourth Industrial Revolution's global span is also unprecedented. Today billions of people are connected through the Internet and mobile devices, creating a huge critical mass that responds by ripple effect to the changes and advancements brought by the emergence of powerful technologies such as robotics, AI, the Internet of things, autonomous vehicles, biotechnology, nanotechnology, three-dimensional (3D) printing and quantum computing, to name just a few.

Many of these technologies have crossed the boundaries of their labs and spread to the consumer market, which in turn provides a huge amount of data, required by technology platform providers, to feed models of human behaviour and manipulate people's choices from what they eat to how they cast their votes.

All industrial revolutions have brought tremendous change and progress to productivity and the quality of human life. There is no reason to think that the fourth digital revolution will not do the same. We should reasonably expect great advancements and improvements to our everyday experience of life, but we should also reflect on potential challengers and threats that such a massive change with so many unknowns can bring about and the disruption to life as we know it.

For modern consumers, technology has provided a highly empowering status reflected in constant access to goods and services that increase effectiveness and enjoyment of our everyday lives. We have music, films, games, information, travel, food and clothes literally at our fingertips.

At the same time, there is increased inequality between the workforce that have technological knowledge, particularly the STEM (science, technology, engineering and mathematics) professions and those who do not. In addition, an increasing number of people all around the world have made exceptional fortunes moving the goal posts for wealth from millionaires to billionaires. Wealth and fortune also ensures the social and political voice and deepens the divide between those who have and those who have not.

In the digital economy, the greatest beneficiaries of technological advancement are innovators, investors and shareholders. This is why income and wealth for the rest of the population has not grown at the same pace – the demand for highly skilled workers has only increased,

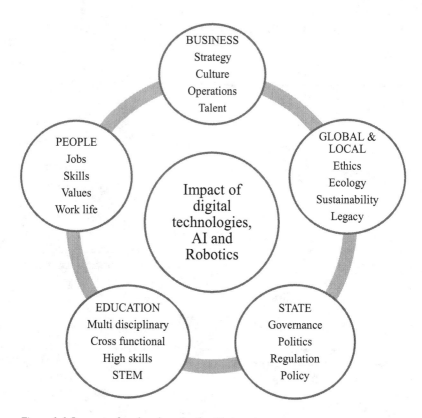

Figure 1.1 Impact of technology in the 21st century

Note: AI = artificial intelligence; STEM = science, technology, engineering and mathematics

resulting in a job market that is also divided. Overall this raises concerns about categories of population in which the current and future generations may actually become poorer than their predecessors. Such division could potentially cause discontent particularly since social media opens the door to a view of how extravagantly some people live, creating unrealistic expectations and aspirations in others.

The impact on people is quite profound because technology affects not only what we do and how we behave as workers and consumers but also our deeper sense of identity. Impacts also include our understanding of ownership, our sense of privacy, the way we balance private life and work, our future careers, the way we plan and develop our skills, how we meet people and establish relationships, the way we manage our health and well-being, the increased use of metrics and quantifications of ourselves and the options we have for human augmentation.

This in turn raises questions about our quintessential human attributes, the way we exercise compassion, make sense of the world and find purpose and meaning in our lives, as we remain permanently connected to our smart phones, which feed us and endless range of information that is fragmented, often contradictory and potentially misleading. The privacy of the information that technology harvests about us is another potential disturbing aspect because it impacts our inner lives and the way we can potentially be seen and judged by others.

All in all, the changes and potential opportunities that are currently pushing out the boundaries of health and longevity, alongside enhanced mental and cognitive capacities, will all demand that we review and redefine our moral and ethical boundaries and standing.

Innovation and disruption also challenge existing economic and business models, whilst leaders are expected to find a new grip on steering and steadying organisations that travel at the great speed of change, to a destination yet to be determined.

Existing needs are now satisfied by new supply and value chains with agile competitors who have access to a global market and digital platforms that enable research, marketing, prototyping, scaling up, sales and distribution. The new supply chains challenge the established suppliers in the field, through alternative offerings of quality, price or speed of delivery, for products and services.

Consumer engagement and experience are powerful drivers in the way companies design and deliver their supplies to meet demand.

Consuming goods and services is also enabled by the shared and on-demand economy that brings together people, assets and data via smart phones. Such platforms weaken the barriers for people and businesses to create wealth, merging the professional and personal spaces of the people who engage in this exchange and as a result create a host of new services from housekeeping to dog walking, from shopping to laundry, parking and travel. At the other end of business, disruptive ways of transacting money totally bypass the financial industry to the tune of millions, whilst alternative set-ups have captured a significant user market.

All in all, it can be said that the transition from the Third to the Fourth Industrial Revolution, from simple digitisation to integration and combination of digitised technologies, is exercising an urgent pressure for businesses to move from what worked in the past but no longer works for the future to a new way of operating starting from fundamentals and all the way thought structure, function, roles, responsibilities, ways of working together and an extreme focus on much needed and coveted skills and capabilities for the future.

Essentially, this industrial revolution has triggered a new and unprecedented review and race for skills and complex sophisticated human talent like never before.

The "in-between" digital enterprise

In the face of significant change, the new structures of global companies had to integrate one other key element of their operation, alongside process and technology, namely, the workforce. The new technology-enabled-businesses had to deal with a number of impacts on real estate and office space, on the challenge of engaging and managing a scattered remote and diverse workforce, of developing new skills, on the way work is regulated and legislated and on the division between those who are technically skilled and those who are not.

The planet has become increasingly integrated, culturally cosmopolitan and economically globalised, with companies worldwide becoming micro-representations of society at large. To keep pace with this new operating model, a new way of company organisation was needed to render it more flexible, nimble and able to respond to market and client requirements faster and more efficiently; hence, the matrix organisation was born. The matrix organisation involves the utilisation of skills (some old, some new and some not even named yet) and resources on a project basis, deploying and re-deploying a company's pool of people, quickly and in accordance with the latest business demand.

The business is, of course, preoccupied by success, which it can achieve by various strategies, such as increasing market share, increasing loyalty of the existing customer base by creating new offerings and advantages and perks that loyal and repeat clients will gain if they stay with the brand, or constantly innovating and diversifying the range of products and services that they offer and so maintain existing clients and increase market share and customer numbers in the process. But to deliver this vision, businesses need people and talent.

Because of their rapid changes in technology and ways of working, the shelf life of skills is decreasing, whilst the turnover of all the new skills is increasing at a pace at which traditional ways of training and development can no longer keep up the pace of demand and supply. This is why organisations need to provide skilling and learning platforms that attract employees to embrace the process of continuous learning and to constantly acquire the skills of the future whilst constantly practising them in the way they work and lead.

Organisations are typically structured around functions and processes, and more often than not, one function does not respect or is not necessarily aware of the activities, value and importance of other functions. In fact, some functions view themselves and their work as being more important than others and so create an internal culture that lacks appreciation for what the other people in the company do. In this scenario, the internal supply and value chain is not very fluid because various functions do not clearly understand the impact of the quality and execution of their specific outputs in the process chain, a chain that exists to the left, right or around their specific position in the process.

This is why the vision for an agile-integrated enterprise cannot be implemented without an appropriate and embodied culture that gathers everyone at work around a clear purpose and guides every individual all the way to the most apparently modest contributor. This vision can be achieved by creating an environment where people work collectively to a common understood higher purpose, are connected and can give feedback and make actual contributions to the business process. In such an environment, people come to work and want to solve important challenges, and they want to do it with smart colleagues.

Regular feedback and direct conversations are mechanisms whereby performance can be recognised, assessed and improved as needed.

The most important aspect of this agile technology–enabled management model is the importance of the feedback loop and the interactive nature between provider and user. In fact, the content of the exchange is effectively co-created by employees who feedback their views, suggestions and solutions in real time, which enables in turn the organisation to prototype, deploy and test solutions quite rapidly. This requires a new way of collaborative work across the value and delivery chain.

Recognition of a team or employee's understanding of the impact that their work has on colleagues and other teams, celebration of successes, lessons learned and continuous improvement are all ways of obtaining and maintaining people's involvement and engagement in achieving, through people and technology combined, what is possible.

The development of artificial intelligence, 3D printing, nanotechnology, genetics, robotics and biotechnology, alongside smart systems for home use, farms, factories or entire cities, will help existing problems, from climate change to supply chain. And the shared economy will increase the power and use of crowdsourcing and increase monetisation across all the range of possible resources, from empty properties to underused vehicles or excessive consumption. All these changes and possibilities are interconnected and amplify each other but also shine a bright light on what is possible; the sky is the limit when people are set to achieve all that can be done or imagined.

Providing a work environment that encourages workers to actively improve customer satisfaction highlights the need for a way of working that has proved to be quite challenging for most organisations. To achieve this, the organisation needs to work across boundaries and across internal silos, as well as extending the understanding of how the internal supply chain of the enterprise has impacts beyond its boundaries into the value chain and ultimately to customers.

People on the two sides of the e-commerce coin

The uptake and success of analogue and digital technologies in everyday life permeated everything in the world of both consumers and employees.

The 1980s was a time of formidable technological advancement that simultaneously brought together personal computers, the Internet and the mobile and later smart phones. In the 1990s, e-commerce grew exponentially alongside an entire services industry and placed consumption, literally, at customers' fingertips. Buying, for millions of people, will never be the same, just as working life, for millions of people, will never be the same again.

The mobile phone has become an alter ego of the human, ubiquitous from the deserts of Africa to the high rises of the USA and Japan, from the quaint villages of France and the UK to the icy poles of the north and south, all around the globe.

What this means is that people can work from home, on weekends, at night, across time zones, all the time or just some of the time. This also means that people today can be both consumers and employees at the same time, all the time.

The digital consumer

On 6 August 1991, the World Wide Web (Internet) became publicly available, and Tim Berners-Lee, now of international fame, posted a brief view of the project on alt.hypertext newsgroup unleashing a technology that dramatically changed the world. The Internet has become an integral part of our lives as a place where everything can be found (from ideas to tangible artefacts), where everyone and anyone can be a content creator and publisher, an open playing field for all.

The Internet is today a convertor of the invisible into actual of all the bright and dark aspects of human nature. It is also a massive source of personal data, which in the digital age is the new and most valuable asset used to exploit and monetise our thoughts, feelings, desires and wants, by the mechanisms of a free market economy based on speculations and profit.

This raises huge ethical and regulatory implications and issues around data ownership, rights, protection, use and distribution and are a permanent feature of daily news. Legislators, platform owners, governments and the police are often unsuccessfully trying to catch up with reality and its unintended consequences, including cyber-crime, trolling and the dark web.

On the other hand, there is also ample evidence on how the Internet and data-based applications are priceless facilitators for individuals to pursue knowledge and convenient consumption, leading to freedom of choices, empowerment and collaborations and open source of ideas that lead to exceptional outcomes. The usefulness and hindrance of the democratised technology driven by AI are mixed up in shades and shadows of unpredictable causality and consequences. They continue to elude clarity and boundaries of governance from the very day they started proliferating some thirty years ago. Again, this shines a light on what it is to be human and how and what we need to do to respect and nurture the deep core of humanity in this digital age.

The Internet has enabled e-commerce, and the power of the consumer today is unprecedented. All businesses that really focus on sustained success pay great attention to what are called the customer journey and the customer experience.

Significantly, the customer has now become the critical feedback factor who has the power to actually determine the way the business operates, its commercial success, its reputation and its overall profitability, whether it is a return to shareholders or to the business itself.

As a result, whatever responsibility we may place on businesses for doing the right thing or the wrong thing, it is a fact that consumers play a big role in the outcome of business strategy and the role businesses play in society at large.

The democratisation of information, access to knowledge, a 24/7 online connectivity culture, the mobile digital devices that are pretty much in every hand of a human inhabiting this planet today and the proliferation of social media platforms and content contribution that the platform users generate have made it possible for customers today to make or break the success of organisations and impact their reputational standing and the bottom line in terms of share prices.

Both businesses and their customers collectively have a responsibility in the space of ethics, sustainability and moral responsibility for the planet, for its resources and for future generations.

However, because a lot of purchases are exercised under impulse and because the advertising and marketing engines are smart and really target the unconscious underbelly of our human nature, it is also understandable how customers may behave in ways that do not help their sustainability and ethical agendas.

The sweet spot in this consumption feedback loop is to find the balance between enabling businesses to offer people a pleasurable experience when they use their income to acquire products or experiences that they either need or want and moderating the volume of offerings and the type of offerings that businesses put out, to satisfy their customers, so that this process of extracting value does not deplete or pollute value.

Responsibility must be shared between those who manufacture and sell and those who buy and discard.

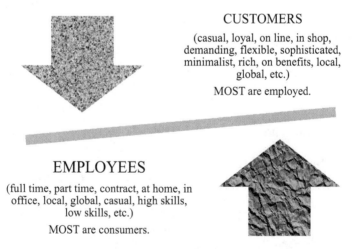

CUSTOMERS

(casual, loyal, on line, in shop, demanding, flexible, sophisticated, minimalist, rich, on benefits, local, global, etc.)

MOST are employed.

EMPLOYEES

(full time, part time, contract, at home, in office, local, global, casual, high skills, low skills, etc.)

MOST are consumers.

Figure 1.2 Digital enterprises in between the people on either side

The digital employee

The world of work post late 1990s has little resemblance to the world of work of even a decade before, and it impacts all aspect of our lives even now. It is also a world that is fragmented and full of contradictions between division of high versus low skills, low and very highly paid jobs, a multitude of ways to deliver work and new challenges to regulation and legislation.

This redefinition of what people do in their work and how work has changed is not new. There have always been vintage skills and skills in high demand related to new technologies. The 1980s was a time of rapid technological advancement that simultaneously brought together personal computers, the Internet and the mobile and later smart phones – a formidable technological triad that enabled an utter transformation in the way people work, including the critical ability to work virtually and globally, with no attachment to a tangible office but rather occupying a virtual transportable place for delivery of skills, from anywhere they are to everywhere they are needed.

The employees of today and the job applicants of tomorrow are children of the virtual world with smart phones and devices hooked 24/7. They are active on social media, in a world that is transparent, filled with information available to all, in quantities much larger than they can ever use. The online world they inhabit is searchable, any question can be answered and any need or desire can be fulfilled, if not immediately and online, then within 24 to 48 hours, as a result of a highly efficient supply and delivery chain that presents to the customers door any possible and imaginable type of product or service.

Today the organisational capability supply chain involves permanent employees, contingent workers, temporary labour, project-based labour and functional resources, working together under various arrangements for pay and benefits and where the volume of employees may be significantly outnumbered by the other categories of people that deliver work to the same organisation.

With everyday life so deeply steeped in technology and virtuality, it is understandable that the same people, as they step through the door into an organisation, business or enterprise, will retain the same expectation in terms of their experience at work, particularly when people spend most of their time at work.

The challenge for businesses is to create a world of work that mirrors in design, technology and experience the world of the consumer today – a world that is dynamic, changing, exciting and developing all the time.

To manage organisational capability, technology is already being used to evaluate and improve performance and skills by way of applications such as the following:

- People analytics: supporting workplace decisions in terms of predicting workforce needs and behaviours, identifying points that need intervention, and ensuring impact of interventions.
- Turning employee experience into a consumer experience: using technology for mobile access, immersive design, gamification and machine learning support that is personalised to individual preferences, in real-time ongoing dialogues with employees, and multimedia multidirectional feedback between central points and individuals.
- Democratising data: opening data to employees to access it themselves, as well as share it via internal networks (intranet, databases, and so on) in terms of availability, skills and achievements, so that a dynamic use of collective capital is enabled around matrix- and project-driven work activities, just like an internal trading platform.
- Real-time ongoing listening, interpreting and feedback: assessing meaning and mood by analysing a large number of individual comments and summarising semantics and then enabling leaders to access this information and to engage with individuals as required, by setting objectives (Workometry analytics, Peakon) or giving real-time feedback continuously (Tap my Back, Zugata) to teams and individuals, related to themes and trends; also making recommendations for developmental needs (Zugata) and updates and improvements.
- Personalised learning by using social platforms: access to personalised skill sets against a role and learning needs; introduction to mentors and others and ways to apply learning (Everwise).
- Cognitive productivity tools: embedded applications (Microsoft Workplace Analytics, Google Goals) that capture an individual's activity levels across a number of communication systems, showing how they are getting the attention of leaders' input and how they are not; as well as drawing leaders' attention to the ratio between intense prolonged focus activity and unstructured time. This ratio can be set, as well as ranked, compared with peers.

This translates into an organisational culture that invests in technology and agile adaptive processes that support its talent by focussing on each individual needs and potential, to profile skills, performance, training and learning needs, developmental and career advancement opportunities, and overall engagement with the community of work.

Appraising enterprise needs and balancing contributions

Prior to the First and Second Industrial Revolutions, the economies of countries around the world depended on agriculture and on small businesses and workshops where goods were produced in small quantities for everyday use or for prestige, art and status. The introduction of mechanised means of production enabled the scaling up of businesses to the tune of tens and hundreds of thousands of people being employed in various businesses. Later some businesses expanded globally and employed hundreds of thousands of people, giving rise to corporations.

Nonetheless, today the economy of most countries is dependent to the tune of around 70% to 80% on small and medium enterprises. Enterprises are usually classified by the number of employees into micro-businesses (fewer than 10 employees) small (10–49 employees) medium (50–249 employees) and large businesses (250–2500 employees) with a turnover – that in the European definitions – does not exceed 50 million euro or an annual balance sheet total less than 43 million euro.

An enterprise is another name for business and describes the activity of people who take initiative and set up, invest and run a business for profit. Around the world, businesses can – broadly speaking – be set up in different ways: sole proprietorships, partnerships, limited liability companies and corporations.

Small medium enterprises (SMEs) represent an important factor in economies, alongside the contribution made by corporations. The fate of SMEs is therefore part of the agenda of governments because they are directly linked to factors such as unemployment, poverty and social stability.

Alongside governments, charities also have an interest in supporting entrepreneurship and successful SMEs for the same reason. This is how the success of small businesses is one point of convergence where governments, charities, the founders and owners of small enterprises and the people that work with them are all aligned in the pursuit of success for broadly the same reasons of economic stability and growth, of wealth generation for the people employed in this economic sector. In the decades following the 1980s, technology has enabled businesses in many ways and has transformed the manner in

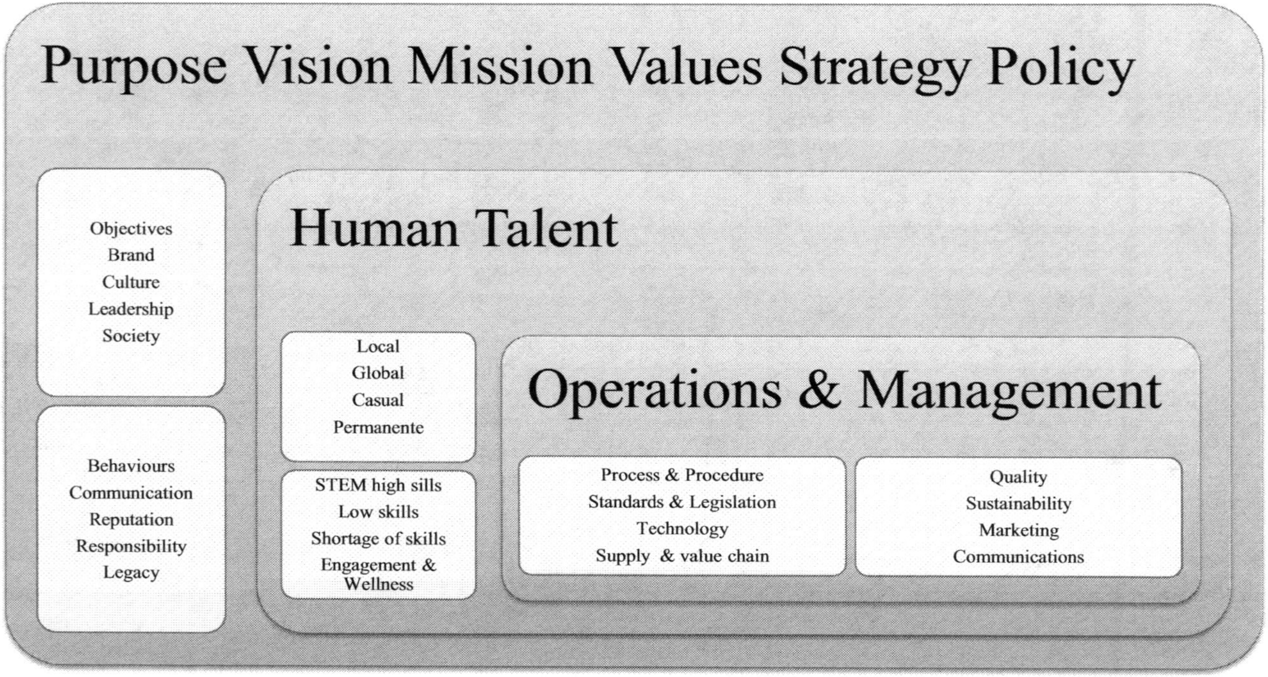

Purpose Vision Mission Values Strategy Policy

Objectives
Brand
Culture
Leadership
Society

Behaviours
Communication
Reputation
Responsibility
Legacy

Human Talent

Local
Global
Casual
Permanente

STEM high sills
Low skills
Shortage of skills
Engagement &
Wellness

Operations & Management

Process & Procedure
Standards & Legislation
Technology
Supply & value chain

Quality
Sustainability
Marketing
Communications

Figure 1.3 Layers of complexity in enterprise dynamics

Note: STEM = science, technology, engineering and mathematics which people can express their creativity and entrepreneurship, at set-up costs that have steadily decreased over time.

The Internet, smart phones and overall office-related technology have all given rise to the virtual office, which completely cut out real estate costs and enables workers to contribute by virtual channels into a converging virtual space, where high-value business can be transacted anytime, anywhere, with anyone, in a potential market of global scale. This has stimulated the appetite of both individuals and governments to encourage entrepreneurship and self-employment through the vehicles of sole trading and founding of small and medium companies.

There are many countries in the world where this model of supporting the so-called smaller players in the economy has worked exceptionally well and where, by the sheer strengths of numbers and quality of the product and services that they deliver, they have firmly placed the reputations of those nations on the global markets. These smaller players are often key providers of, typically, components and elements that contribute to the creation of much larger outputs, somewhere else, in countries that have been set up as large hubs for manufacturing or provision of services.

This is why supporting the set-up and development of SMEs remains a very hot topic into which governments, charities and inspirational successful individuals invest their energy.

More than ever before and because today we can set up companies with low initial investment, there is appetite on both sides of the enablers and the implementers to come together and develop economies where everyone's contribution is successful. But the failure rate of small companies remains high at around 60% to 80%, and the good ideas that start up a new business are not sufficient for business to stay alive or at least break even two years after inception.

A lot of energy invested in starting up and attempting to rapidly grow a business through aggressive sales strategies with not enough operational capability to actually deliver the high quality promised goes to waste because of a number of well-researched reasons that some eighteen to twenty-four months later brings the business down.

Paying attention to growth and operational infrastructure that the small business requires for success in the longer run goes hand in hand with knowledge and experience around business management that often entrepreneurs and founders do not have. Furthermore, they may lack a roadmap to follow to acquire the mandatory skills and capabilities that their organisation should have to be successful. What follows are business examples that clearly demonstrate the

complexity of a business enterprise that exists behind the simple statement "I have a friend who makes cookies from home, and she's been
very successful in selling them," as an example.

Complex management capabilities and vision are necessary in every enterprise regardless of size

At first glance, a cookie-making business may seem simple enough,
and we may think quite rightly that there are big differences in the
way a business run with three people or with two thousand people
actually works. And yet – differences of scale which indeed bring in
additional complexities notwithstanding – from the point of view of
the range of activities that need to be performed, there are few differences. To illustrate this, here are two examples that come to mind of
people I know.

The first example is that of Michelle, who is a mother of three,
a wife and a cookie maker, passionate about engaging in an activity which she enjoys and which also generates an income, working
from home.

Michelle started a small business making cookies from home. The
idea came to her as a result of two factors: (1) she had a very good recipe that she learned from her grandmother, and (2) she made cookies
and took them to her children's school for various school activities.

Her homemade cookies were very much appreciated; people asked
where she got them because they would have liked to buy the cookies
themselves.

This gave her the idea that if she would make her special cookies
in larger quantities and take them to the local community and the
groups of people where she was known, she would have a market that
was ready to buy. This was the beginning of her enterprise, and the
rest, as they say, is history.

But beyond the simple tale that is not uncommon for the way small
businesses start – with a good idea! – there is a business process worth
analysing, one that Michelle may have not articulated in formal business language.

In fact, Michelle needed to:

> Assess her ability to produce larger quantities of product and
> establish what number of cookies she could bake within a day and
> whether she had the space in her kitchen to actually make them.
>   Analyse what volume of ingredients she now needed to buy to
> create larger quantities of cookies and whether she could ensure

the supply of the ingredients at better prices because she was buying raw materials in bulk.

Ensure that she could get childcare from her parents on the days when she had larger orders to fulfil and could not personally take care of her children.

In addition, she considered whether she could deliver the cookies herself or she could strike a deal with a small delivery company, which she would contract for a number of days a month for a more advantageous price to deliver to her clients.

Based on this analysis of costs, resources and time involved in her scaling up her cookie production from a small amount that she baked for her own consumption to a larger quantity that could fulfil orders coming from clients that would order for functions or for catering, she was able to put together a business plan and a cash flow requirement, create necessary supply alliances for her raw materials and delivery services and free time for her to fulfil larger orders whilst ensuring childcare by her parents who – being retired – were only too glad to look after their grandchildren.

The success in this case was based on the fact that she had a product that the market liked; she could establish supply chains around raw materials and the delivery of finished products; she had a marketing channel, including online and personal referrals; and she did not disrupt her personal life or neglected her role as a mother and wife because she had support from her family.

In this context, given the financial support, the personal support, the good supply chain, relationships and the strong brand reputation that she represented herself, as well as the infrastructure at home where she had a sufficiently large kitchen to bake and then pack her products her enterprise was quite successful quite swiftly.

On close scrutiny, Michelle is involved in a complex business processes that involves manufacturing, combines both products and services and needs attention to the quality of materials as well as the relationships across the entire supply and value chain.

She also has an additional special benefit in that whilst she appears to be working alone in her business, she receives critical voluntary support from her family, so she saves money that she would otherwise have to pay. She also has peace of mind in the knowledge that childcare and overall support are delivered by people she knows and loves.

Regarding the future prospects of her business, it is a matter of deciding what is it that she wants to do with this business in the future. She may decide to keep it going as it is and simply fulfil the purpose of her own enjoyment as well as generating a moderate but steady revenue. She may equally consider that her cookie business is actually not only a food business but could also cross into a gift business, too, and diversify by developing special packaging and special recipes and a specific line of products that would be suitable as gifts for special occasions and which could be personalised, demand a higher price and potentially grow and diversify her business at the same time.

This would, of course, require careful planning of cash flow and increased involvement with other subcontractors in the supply chain for the design and manufacturing of special packaging, for example. She may decide to keep the product line as it is but scale up the volume and expand her delivery not only in the local area but also throughout the country or indeed internationally.

Again, this will require careful consideration of cash flow, the risks, the need for additional specialist skills (e.g., website creation) and international deliveries, as well as the actual setup of her manufacturing base, which is her home kitchen. But what this apparently simple example of a one-person enterprise demonstrates is that the individual owner and sole trader is in fact responsible for a long list of activities, which we may call organisational functions, that range all the way from pricing, invoicing and advertising to manufacturing and logistics, not forgetting financial management, tax returns and quality control, all these in the context of her personal circumstances being that of a mother of three children and a provider of care to her family which she loves.

A simple small business apparently unsophisticated that can be run in one's pyjamas from one's home kitchen is in fact a rather complicated affair filled with responsibility and the need for a diverse range of skills that have to be provided, either by the one sole trader or by resources – voluntary or paid – who are involved in the good running of the enterprise.

In the second example I know, this is a business based in London, providing accommodation for visitors coming from Asia to Europe. This is an example of a service-based business that nonetheless has got implementation aspects on the ground.

Initially, Jane, the founder of the business, had the idea of offering this service because she noticed that there is a need in the market to link the clients from Asia with accommodation in Italy.

So Jane identified the client base, identified a city where the clients wanted to visit and identified the need of providing accommodation other than a hotel.

Whilst an online service, in fact, Jane had to identify and lock in, in Italy, the relevant stock of accommodation plus a group of people, on the ground, who could provide cleaning, maintenance and repairs during and in between client stays.

In this case, Jane also needed a customer support linked to her online offer as well as online payment facilities that were secure.

Starting from an excellent idea which proved to be successful and in which her service offer had a strong online front-end presence, she also needed, from an implementation point of view, to set up an operational delivery capability that involved a different set of skills and people.

Clearly, this was an international business because her clients, the offering and the head office and support centre were located in a different country. In addition, the range of skills that she utilised to deliver this model of services ranged from unskilled and low skilled to very highly skilled (e.g., cleaners, trades people, IT specialists, online marketing specialists, call centre agents and overall management able to oversee both operations and IT functions).

Again, having started her business from home, she soon enough had to move to an office; hire more people, not only in London but also in Italy; and find ways to supervise the quality of work delivered, manage people and deal with quite a set of complexities that moved her from being a one-person business to having staff in two countries and the keys to many properties for which she was responsible.

Comparing the two businesses, there are a few aspects which immediately become apparent in terms of level of complexity, geographic settings, range of skills, the importance of technology in the business success, risks, size of resources and ability to control quality throughout the entire supply chain, to name just a few. They are all just as present in small businesses as they are in large organisations or corporations except that the scale, risk, resilience, assets, cash flow and resources in general as well as governance and quality of processes differ and, in my view, are much less robust in small enterprises. If one person does not do their job in company of two hundred people, there are always colleagues that can fill that gap, but in a business of one or three or ten, the negative impact is really serious and the recovery much slower and costly.

For example, in the cookie-making business, the person who had the idea was also able to herself produce and even deliver the product. Therefore, the quality of the product was assured because she was the only person involved in the creation of the product from idea to customer experience, with whom Michelle was able to personally engage to get feedback and then put into practice whatever suggestions were made to develop new products or improve the initial one.

The overall important thing in the cookie-making business is the fact that the level of control of the person who generated the idea over the entire business process is almost 100%, and even if Michelle were to increase her resources by hiring additional people to bake more cookies, it still allows her to control the quality of the product and monitor this scaling up quite closely.

Michelle can also provide guidance mentoring and supervision to another cookie makers who could potentially work alongside her. Therefore, the risk in this business is quite low and is directly linked to the behaviour and the performance of the person who had the initial idea and implemented it.

By the same token, business continuity or scaling up can quite easily be assured personally by the founder.

The service business, on the other hand, is completely different with a much greater level of complexity risk, dependencies and potential variation in quality assurance.

The fact that the person who originated the idea can only implement one limited aspect of the operational delivery of that service makes this business much more vulnerable.

As an owner and idea generator, Jane effectively depends on the services delivered to her by every single one of the other people who are involved in that business from the cleaners who keep the flats tidy and ready to receive new guests to the IT professionals who have built her online presence and payment systems and could provide to her business skills that are critical and which she cannot exercise herself.

She may well be able, for example, to clean flats or even repair simple things in those locations except that she herself lives in another city, so she is not physically present at the point of delivery to either be able to personally supervise the local activity or roll up her sleeves and step in to take up some of the simpler jobs that she may be able to do herself on the ground.

Therefore, in this case, the success of Jane's business is fully dependent on one specific skill that she could hopefully be able to exercise herself, namely, that of setting the vision and the quality standards as the business leader and managing interdependencies and relationships from a strategic perspective by establishing connections with all her subcontractors who are located remotely.

The strength of her presence and her visibility in the business across all geographies that include her head office in London her potential clients in north America and the people who look after the properties in Italy has to be credible, motivational, sustained and effective. She would also have the option to hire managers on the ground to act as motivational supervisors.

It is clear that the amount of input that she actually needs to deliver the service is quite significant, and as the business grows, the scaling up of the business structure becomes more complex and more differentiated, including the need for at least one additional layer of management between herself and the people who deliver their specific business objectives.

There are other ways to compare businesses not only in terms of where the main risks and efforts are but also in terms of scale.

For example, at the other end of the magnitude scale in Michelle's cookie-making business, there are Cadbury (established in 1824, in England, today operating in 50 countries, employing more than 50,000 employees) and Mars Inc. (started in 1911, USA, operating internationally and employing thousands).

Cadbury and Mars Inc. have been running successfully for decades, employing a significantly larger number of people, and more important, working with quantities and turnovers that run into tons and millions. In addition, the level of automation in these manufacturing bases that put out tens of thousands of individual sweets per day is extremely high and sophisticated.

In Michelle's case, what she generates in financial terms is the equivalent of a sufficient and moderate salary if she were to be employed. She only provides employment for herself. In the case of Cadbury and Mars, the financial numbers run into millions, and the people employed run into tens of thousands. Additionally, these companies each have a very complicated global supply chain served by distribution networks and warehousing. The workings of such a global operation are also highly visible because of their impact on many people and other systems. Understandably, they are also subject to public scrutiny, which holds them accountable for various aspects of compliance and ethics.

In Jane's case, she generates an income for herself, but she also has to ensure an income for all the people she employees, totalling twenty people, in two countries, and the number of employees may well increase if she increases the number of available accommodation that she can offer. An increased offering would also increase the number of people who need to look after those residences and the number of people in support functions such as marketing and IT-related resources.

A similar model scaled up may look like Airbnb or a chain of hotels such as Holiday Inn (first hotel opened in 1952, with more than 1,000 hotels and resorts around the world today) or Hilton (first hotel bought in 1919, toady with more than 570 hotels and resorts in eighty five countries on six continents). The financial and operational implications in these scaled-up examples are self-explanatory in terms of costs and revenue streams running all the way up to millions. Whilst the scale is very different, both businesses have to perform well the same intricate business functions.

The most important thing for us here is to acknowledge that in all cases, there are fundamental functions, principles and categories of resources and activities that are identical. This is to serve the point that there are no differences between the business of one person and a business employing 800 or 200,000 people when it comes to necessary project management, people, financial and quality management aspects for the same type of business, regardless whether it is small, medium, large or corporate.

Fundamentally, all businesses deal with planning resources, managing customer relationships and managing the supply chain. There are systems available today to automate and oversee these categories of activities in the following enterprise management systems:

- ERP: Enterprise Resource Planning
- CRM: Customer Relationship Management
- SCM: Supply Chain Management

Because of the online presence that almost every business today has, one other aspect to consider is the development of an enterprise-level search engine optimisation (SEO) strategy and best practice, which reflects the needs of the enterprise. This requires attention paid to the following aspects:

- Working with other departments or collaborators
- Brand and multichannel engagement
- Scale (can be an advantage or a disadvantage)
- Cross-channel marketing
- Data

An enterprise of any size must pay attention to all fundamentals, but the difference in scale naturally brings in additional challenges, not so much by the magnitude and value of assets that different size businesses acquire and manage but by the number of people that the business needs to run successfully.

So the critical factor is about how to successfully manage one person, ten people or 200,000 people.

Tangible assets owned by a business can be acquired or divested and are devoid of any dynamic of their own and stay where they are and as they are, being passive in the hands of ownership and management.

People, on the other hand, are obviously a live, dynamic force, volatile, with minds of their own, who question, agree or disagree, support or sabotage, become absorbed or disinterested and are defined by a high degree of unpredictability because people are a self-transforming and moving target.

This is why scaling up a business that involves increasing the number of employees also increases the demand for care to be exercised around human talent and engagement. When everything that can be done is being done, the chance of predicting a good and desired outcome related to people's involvement and output at work still remains relatively low. A significant effort towards high-quality people and talent management may still yield a low return on expectations or, for a particular individual or team, may return more than expected against a moderate effort.

In science, what is true for large statistical numbers is not necessarily applicable in every individual case or scenario. But overall, it is true to say that because of the complex and unpredictable quality of human nature, the mystery of how a certain input may pan out into what type of output remains uncertain. Meanwhile, the workings of the black box in between is still being unravelled by research and science as ongoing work in progress.

When we accept that businesses cannot run without people and that people require constant sophisticated attention even when happy and inspired by the best management, they may still respond in ways that are below expectations despite the initial effort invested. Equally, if we do not pay enough attention to the people factor, we undermine the very core of the business' existence.

Doing one's best to look after people in organisations, setting expectations and helping them to be achieved is the best model to guarantee results. Attracting, engaging, developing and rewarding people in organisations with the full understanding and belief that they are the key to success even if people are much harder to look after and even if the reward for that investment may not be exactly what we would ideally want.

Therefore, just as we have fundamental business functions that are present in every business regardless of its size, we also have fundamental

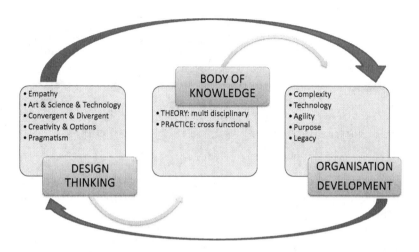

Figure 1.4 People-focussed enterprise design, body of knowledge and development

needs in people that have to be attended to. As an absolute baseline a business must have respect for and satisfy human nature before anything else that has to be added. This means, as an absolute must, paying attention to the work environment, skills, technology, processes and general infrastructure, all important aspects and enabling factors for the fundamentals of a business.

For example, we need not bring arguments to the statement that generally people like to be treated nicely instead of being treated aggressively or prefer a smile to a frowning face.

This just brings to mind an example of the coffee shop chain where the first and immediate criterion for selection in the recruitment process is whether the candidates, as they walk through the door of the interviewing room, smile or not. One may think this is a superficial criterion to use, and it may well be, but in an environment where service to customers is quite close up and personal and where staff and clients constantly look each other in the eye, separated by a distance of only a few metres, it becomes a self-sustaining argument that a staff member with a friendly, open, smiling face creates a welcoming and pleasant interaction with the customer.

The positive emotions exchanged between smiling employees and happy customers tickle our hardwired need for cohesion, inclusiveness and collaboration and offer a foundation layer to the recipe for a flourishing business.

People make the place and what may go wrong when they don't

It has been decades since I started in my first job, and the world has changed and moved on in many ways because of technology, labour legislation and new organisation structures and business processes. However, some things have not moved at all, and today I am disappointed to continue to hear so many negative stories from people I meet in my work.

These stories reflect an ongoing lack of respect and care for basic civilised human interaction, lapses, in my view, utterly unnecessary and totally avoidable. These examples also show the distance that we have to cover to move reality closer to the vision of what "good looks like" and how facts on the ground undermine the vision when it comes to business cultures and people in business. This is in spite of modern and quite advanced business set-ups that often leave the applied leadership, values and behaviours on the ground, behind.

Valuing the customers above potential employees
and potential useful talent

Recently, a friend of mine was looking for a job and had been to a number of interviews, just as one does when looking for a job. His overall experience was negative, and he was really disgusted with the fact that communication and updates between him and potential employers and recruiters lacked any respect for him and his activity in the job market. He made a bitter and poignant remark, saying that none of these companies would have ever dared to treat their customers in the way they treated him. He made the point that it was not the positive outcome of his interviews that was concerning but the utter lack of respect throughout the process in which he was treated more like an inconvenience than a valued candidate.

Yet all he was doing was interacting with companies around the possibility of providing his skills, expertise and professionalism to be put to use by an employer. In his eyes, quite rightly, those potential employers clearly discriminated between candidates and customers, without thinking that the job candidates are potentially people who eventually become employees and deliver goods and products to the very customers that they appear to respect.

One rule for some and not the same for others

Another example comes to mind from an employee working in a reputable global firm that has all the necessary business sophistication, including mentoring and internal career progression programs in place. This person told me about her monthly debriefing sessions with her counsellor, whose presumed role was to mentor her and facilitate her career in the organisation. All these discussions were around her efforts and were yet another demand for her to adjust and be even more collaborative, more flexible and more productive in her role.

However, to her, honest and open comments regarding senior partners in the firm, who were treating others with disrespect by not providing them with timely information, making demands on their time outside working hours at weekends and late into the night, were met with the cynical comment that such things are not going to change. The conclusion of the counsellor was that she was the one who was "struggling" because she couldn't consistently work into the middle of the night or sustain meaningful conversations with senior staff who would call her from cars and on the move, with poor Wi-Fi connections and reception, where she frankly told me, she simply couldn't hear what they were saying.

The hypocrisy and double standards the organisation had for those who were diligent and worked hard, being asked to work even harder and for those behaving badly being allowed to continue to do so with no attempt to make them develop or change, is without a doubt, to any reasonable thinker, utterly unacceptable, particularly when the unfairness favours managers, owners, partners or directors who should be modelling the best behaviours required of others. Such discrimination is not uncommon in large organisations, which paradoxically, also have some of the best systems for training and development in place. Yet power, status and authority seem to remain a challenge in practice when it comes to a level playing field for all.

The peculiar culture of some small businesses

In another example, someone told me about his work as a human resources (HR) recruiter for a fast-growing start-up managed by a founder who had instated a so-called closely knit culture in his small business. For example, people were expected to have lunch together every day, so much so that daring to take one's lunch break outside the office lunch table was regarded with suspicion and interpreted as a betrayal of the extended family feel that he was effectively trying to impose.

In addition, the founder brought his wife and a relative into the business. Staff found themselves caught in the middle of the influence and power games being played within the owner's close circle, resulting in factions and encouraging gossip and eavesdropping. At the same time, the founder constantly undermined the professional expertise of the people he hired, including my colleague, on the grounds that, as their boss, he knew better. This was an utter travesty of work relations with no boundaries between private and public; between professional fields of expertise and personal ego; between roles, status and responsibilities; between management, ownership and technical specialism.

Needless to say, being treated most of the time like a child whilst also being pressured as professionally accountable for his work, in spite of being undermined by hierarchical posturing, turned the feel of the business into a kind of feudal servitude. Understandably, this lack of clarity of role, status, responsibility and misaligned authority caused great stress to many of the people working there, including my colleague.

Such unprofessional work relations, dressed in the so-called "friendly extended family culture" were in fact toxic, so much so that years after my colleague's six-month contract, he still vividly remembers that stress, alongside a fear of and determination never to land into a similar kind of manipulative and disempowering workplace again.

Conflicts of interests, politics and the power of manipulation

Considerations over the recent experiences of people I know well also brought to mind memories of my own experiences decades ago. Thinking back to my own life at work and the number of situations that I have also encountered, I am saddened to see that even though the world of work has moved on a lot in the past few decades, there are yet so many things that have not changed at all.

I remembered a situation when – some two decades ago, in an otherwise excellent organisation – my direct line manager was also acting as my counsellor and coach, which led us to conversations about how I felt in my role, the things I liked or disliked and the way I perceived that my skills and talents did or did not match the role description as well as the shortcomings of the actual role. I tend to be quite honest and open, and in those days I was much younger and not politically astute. This manager in her own right had been with the company for many, many years and had been able to maintain her role and status in spite of the fact that she was an average performer. She was particularly skilled at hiding her lack of real competence by using a particular strategy which I eventually noticed and which, I realised, was incredibly effective.

Her main activity consisted of receiving, sending, endorsing, supporting or acknowledging communications that contained calls to action or decision making. However, what she actually did not do was to take action, make decisions or involve herself in any active way when required to provide technical expertise or managerial decisions. Sitting at the centre of this communications hub, she monitored the traffic, never responding to emails, allowing a good deal of time and other forces to work before replying with an profuse apology plus the question whether the situation had been resolved or could she help in some way and how, always at the precise moment when she knew that things had been picked up by other people.

I remember looking at the time at her emails, which were simply a long string of apologies and empty words, noticing the pattern and that there was something very wrong in that picture. Yet in those days, I was unable to understand and articulate the fact that this was a skilled and deeply manipulative person playing perception games and maintaining her safe place in the organisation.

Being a person who focussed on the task and always took responsibility for myself and my work, I did not realise then that in a large company with strong resources and a wide network of people involved in various tasks and responsibilities, if one waited long enough, all requests around a problem will eventually disappear because sooner or later, someone within the system will step in and directly or indirectly impact outcomes that would resolve or eliminate the problem raised in the first place.

But I've learned from observing this woman at work, who was doing no work, that if one waits long enough – in a large system of interconnected resources – things tend to eventually sort themselves out, and one can take credit for the resolution or simply linger in the quiet waters of noninvolvement, with no contribution and no responsibility, and get nicely paid for it, with no dent on one's reputation. Needless to say, my relationship with her, whilst superficially collaborative and with a lot of foolish honesty on my side, didn't pan out very well for me. Being the naïve party in this game, the moment an opportunity arose, she used all the private and confidential information that I exchanged with her against me.

Her lack of competence or refusal to provide it when needed, her breach of trust and confidentiality exercised from position of power and her lack of interest and empathy towards the people she used as means to an end are examples of how some people play the organisation to their advantage.

Manipulation and political astuteness to her credit, she was very able to stay where she wanted to be, maintaining good pay and status successfully and for decades, in spite of professional mediocrity and low contribution, if any, to the organisational effort.

The bully in the ranks

Another example that came to mind was that of working as part of the internal audit and business process re-engineering activity in a highly competent team producing software for a very large client. The team was put together by collecting some seven people, all self-directed subject matter specialists in different domains, under the supervision of a project leader.

My relationship with my colleagues was excellent because we were all highly professional independent workers who did not need close or direct supervision and used our expertise to guide others. But for our project leader, this was a long-awaited opportunity to acquire a new shiny feather in his cap, with the potential for some kind of promotion or acknowledgement on which he was very keen. This made him constantly assert his status and not necessarily welcome inputs on process and content from his peers – the team – whom he treated like subordinates, positioning himself as top person and ultimate expert.

Again, in my naïve way, I expressed some alternatives on my own activities with suggestions of doing my work differently. He invited me to a private meeting and directly threatened me, stating that if I did not stop commenting and having my own ideas about this work, he would exercise his privilege around my performance appraisal and potential salary review.

I was shocked and angry, and whilst I lacked the subtleties of political machinations I certainly had a strong sense of right and wrong and the energy to fight back – no matter the risks – so I reported his threats to HR. I do not know what conversations took place between HR and him, but what I know is that we all went back to business as usual with the difference that I could make my suggestions without being antagonised or shut up, whilst our project leader demonstrated more flexibility to constructive input not only from me but also from my colleagues.

His performance review of my work was also submitted to a second manager and evaluated according to merit and not only his version of how good my work was. What also helped was that I had an already established and recognised reputation as a subject matter specialist and a history of happy and productive collaborations with many managers and peers who valued me prior to this particular incident.

Negative personal experiences disengage people even in good organisations

Following a rather enjoyable (a rare occurrence) recruitment process, I was hired to an ideal role, to work with a wonderful boss, only to find a few months later that he was promoted to another role, and a new boss came in to lead our team. This man was definitely dull and unskilled in building relationships with the people he worked most closely with and was technically mediocre. But he had been with the company for many, many years and clearly knew how to play politics and change roles and environments within the company so that he assured his status and income.

His problem was, of course, that on the one hand, he needed the expertise of his team to make him look good, and he used it when he presented to his bosses as well as other departments. But he resented the fact that his subordinates could potentially be smarter or more knowledgeable than him. In the individual conversations that he had with us, when we were required to provide him with information for his reporting and updates, he used every possible opportunity to make us feel little and put us in our place, whilst appropriating our expertise that was useful for him to look good. Again, this was not something that I could tolerate gladly, so our relationship was tense, to say the least.

Because this was a matrix organisation, I very soon started looking for opportunities and quickly found the possibility of working on a special business-critical and strategic project. I applied for that role, and because its visibility was high and it was a regional and global rollout of a new business model, the project needed expertise fast. My boss could not block me from leaving his department and transferring, without the risk of being seen to be obstructive to critical global business ambitions.

Clearly, we both knew that the reason I was moving was because of the strained relationship between us, and he clearly wasn't happy with the fact that he lost the resource which was instrumental in providing information that sat within his area of responsibility and which he needed to report upstream monthly. But our smouldering conflict came to a happy end for me.

Ironically, I only moved to the other side of the same large open plan office when taking up the new role and joining the new project manager and team, just a few metres away from what had been a place of bitterness. This job turned out to be one of the most exciting, stimulating, successful and enjoyable work experiences of my life.

What is wrong with this wider picture of unnecessary bad experience of employees in organisations is that my recollections go back to the 1990s, but the examples coming from others date to 2018 and 2019. For almost three decades of time, during which without any doubt tremendous positive changes have taken place not only in organisations but also the wider regulatory and legislative systems, the culture and some practices on the ground have not changed at all.

On balance, it is also true that then just as today, there have been and there are options and possibilities to find better personal outcomes within the same business or elsewhere, and people do move on, often leaving organisations because of immediate negative work relationships, usually with the boss. This again repositions the question, why should we accept bad management and normalise bitter experiences for people who are motivated to work well for the greater enterprise goals?

Such pressures are a tremendous and unnecessary waste of potential and opportunities for all involved. If only we respected people and paid proper attention to people's happiness in business. All we need to do is really embrace and actually use on the ground the fit for purpose selection of means out of the significant amount of remedial options offered by enterprise design and development methodologies and the multidisciplinary and cross-functional bodies of knowledge that are available to us.

Bibliography

Executive Office of the President of the United States, National Science and Technology Council Committee on Technology (Oct. 2016). *Preparing for the future of artificial intelligence.*

Lane, A. D. and Corrie, S. (2006). *The modern scientist-practitioner.* Oxford: Routledge.

Tarry, A. (2018). *Coaching with careers and AI in mind: grounding a hopeful and resourceful self fit for a digital world.* Abingdon: Routledge.

2 New perspectives on adaptive responses

With a level playing field for all – just like with information technology in the last four decades – competition and commercial edge will be gained not by the technology itself, but by how well technology serves human needs and the quality of human experience.

Adina Tarry, *Coaching with Careers and AI in Mind*

People at the centre of a new order enterprise and why design thinking is fit for this purpose

Design has its origins in creativity methods as a part of many different fields of activity such as engineering, architecture, crafts and urban planning; in more recent times, it has also been used in interior decoration and the mass production of consumer goods.

Initially, design was considered an art, and art could be defined as a range of human activities that enable an author to express imagination and ideas by the production of works that appeal to our senses and have the quality of moving us emotionally and enchant us through attributes of beauty. Art has also been philosophically and historically considered as having a connection with the irrational, with emotion, with divine inspiration, with imitation, with sensibility and generally with manipulation of mood and use of symbolism to trigger an immediate, intimate, personal response in the people who witness it.

The difference between art and commercial art or craft and design as applied arts resides in the fact that art needs to convey, beyond its aesthetic form or commercial value or practical use, a deeper essence that relates to thought, meaning, beliefs and feelings potentially connected to messages of a higher order about our human nature. Art engenders commonly shared human spirituality and beliefs and enhances the power to create a level of collectively accepted order within social groups.

Each person takes out of art what suits them. However, people are also moved collectively and reassured by a sense of fraternity and collective belonging. Art may speak to each individual but also speaks to all individuals at the same time, at the most accessible, deep and primitive level of a collective experiential immersion.

In addition to incorporating art, design also means creating something that can be used easily and effectively to accomplish the task for which that particular product or service has been initially envisioned. Therefore, good design is also about functionality effectiveness fitness for purpose and elegance with appeal to the aesthetic sensibilities of the time.

Having held this position of art and functionality for many centuries, the notion of design saw a metamorphosis in the 1960s, when it gained the focus of attention in its own right as a professional discipline, so much so that by 2015, it transformed from a method related to creativity into a formalised and transferable discipline in its own right, known as "design thinking".

In this context, design also acquired an association with science. Originally, the word *science* was used to define a particular type of knowledge, for instance, knowledge about the workings of natural things that people could communicate to each other and share. In its modern sense, science is defined as the systematic structure of knowledge in testable ways that enable explanations and predictions about the universe.

From the mathematics, astronomy and medicine of 3000 BC, to the natural philosophy of the Greek antiquity, to the scientific method of the 16th century, science today is mainly divided into three different branches: natural sciences, which broadly study nature such as physics, chemistry and biology; formal sciences, which study abstract concepts such as mathematics, logics and computer sciences; and the social sciences, which study individuals and societies, such as psychology, sociology and economics.

One could argue that the purpose of design was also to use available knowledge and apply it to various new and diverse environments – well beyond the initial association with arts and crafts to make things large and small, a position held for many centuries – and open it up to a much wider utilisation.

By the 1980s, design thinking was associated with a practice applicable to situations of uncertainty, variability, uniqueness and value conflict. Design thinking found application in Six Sigma streamlining design for quality control. In the 1990s, academics and practitioners in Europe and the US developed a theory and practice for design thinking to solve the so-called "wicked problems" or intractable human concerns through design.

The early 2000s saw the extrapolation of design thinking into business with a remit to creating a more design-focussed workplace where innovation could thrive.

By 2015, design thinking was taught as a discipline in engineering, formal design education programs were established and design thinking was introduced in the design of services.

Today it is accepted that design is both an art and science and can be applied in both domains and in recent times also in social and business contexts. This is because business and social systems are complex and dynamic and filled with problems in which the questions and the solutions are both ill defined, presenting us with "wicked problems". Solving them requires adaptive expertise, choosing the right inflection points and the appropriate next steps. Implementing this level of design thinking requires an iterative, higher order intellectual process that needs to be learned and practised.

Today design, in its "design thinking" form, is no longer merely a craft-based skill but is instead a knowledge-based discipline in its own right, backed by research and practice, with a rigorous process, methods, principles, language, domains of applications and thinking strategies.

Introduction to the design process

The design thinking process differs from the milestone-based linear approach that is typically used in problem solving. This is why it may seem chaotic at times – because the various steps of the process may loop back, be repeated or occur simultaneously. Design thinking taps into a human capacity that is often not utilised in typical (waterfall) problem-solving practices, namely, creating overlapping and concurrent spaces that enabled the team to explore new directions and refine the collectively generated ideas (heuristics, hunches, imaginings) through iteration. This process eventually leads to clarity even if it achieves this result by taking a different non-linear path, something that artificial intelligence (AI) of today, for example, can only "dream" about. The design thinking process typically includes five main stages – that may themselves branch out, intertwine and include other sub-stages – before full implementation:

1   Inspiration or understanding the opportunity or problem is the first phase of the design thinking process. This initial understanding can be framed by a number of constraints, benchmarks and

objectives to be realised, all of which define the parameters of the problem or opportunity.

2   Empathising with the users is mandatory and exercised quite early in the process because it informs the designers about the needs and wants of the design beneficiaries and how the designers might use technology and mixed knowledge to improve the experience of those who would use the outcome of the design. This needs to match their psychological and emotional needs and fit with their view of the world and what is meaningful to them.

3   The third phase is ideation or generating ideas by brainstorming and thinking outside the box, going wide as far as possible in terms of multiple concepts, outcomes and options, without judgement. This is achieved by using both divergent and convergent thinking in multidisciplinary teams where specialists and polymaths contribute their knowledge across different fields. Eventually, ideas that survive scrutiny in line with the design brief rise to the surface, and the synthesis that follows eventually leads to potential solutions to achieving the goal.

4   Prototyping is the next step following the generation of viable ideas and represents turning ideas into something concrete that enable testing, iteration and refinement of the project. The prototype helps with gathering feedback that is essential for improvement because it provides an opportunity to understand the strengths and weaknesses of the new solution. This is also a step when testing, failure change and retest follow and can be afforded because the cost of losses is much lower than when a product may be scaled up and be found to be inadequate.

5   Testing prototypes in situations and environments of restricted resources when infrastructure, communication and support are limited contributes to creating a product or service that is much more robust and potentially suitable for difficult or undeveloped markets.

Successful prototyping and testing leads to scaling up the implementation of the new solution that has been created by the inspiration and empathy stages.

Design thinking and its focus on people, "wicked problems" and complex dynamic environments make it fit for the digital age.

Definitions of an enterprise present us with the fact that an enterprise is made of many things, in themselves complex subsystems that come together to create an enterprise. The enterprise as an entity fulfils a purpose and a mission, set by its reason of being and by the leaders that map its path in terms of purpose, mission, vision and objectives, projected over a period of time. But there are companies today that indeed have a mission statement for decades ahead and others that do not have one at all; finding the balance in between rests in really understanding how defining a purpose can actually help a business in focussing its activity.

Enterprises are also defined as part of the wider society, structures where people deliver a certain type of activity usually around skills that they provide in exchange for recognition including financial remuneration.

We can also define enterprises as a combination of technology, processes, people, culture and leaders that come together to achieve something that has been planned or envisioned.

A place of work is something that almost everyone is likely to experience in their lives; some experiences will be good, and others will not be so good. All workplaces have certain characteristics; many of these are unique to the workplace and can be very demanding, and overall, a place of work is also different from other experiences that we may have in social settings.

Human beings join social settings as soon as they are born. First there is the immediate group of family, relatives, carers and friends. Later we move on to increasingly wider circles represented by the institutions that our society has set up, some thousands of years old. Such structures host different types of activities such as education, governing bodies, leisure, entertainment and work. There are differences between the expectations of those who frequent them as well as the rules and dynamics that define each of them. Education and work are activity types which are most prevalent in human societies, and typically they follow in a certain succession. Whilst both require of us participation and contribution, they are quite different.

Educational establishments such as schools and other technical or higher education institutions are environments that present a certain level of routine-based stability and clarity with respect to roles and responsibilities. They offer opportunities to establish relatively stable relationships with other children and young people over time, as well as between students and teachers. And the formative impact of these years can be quite significant for future development.

Such an experience may often add up to some eight years of continuity within the same setting and the same group of people, peers and adults. In higher education, the length of time spent by students in universities is somewhat shorter, between three and five years, but the same stability of fellow students, lecturers, tutors and supervisors applies. This is how up to sixteen years or so of our early life is spent in what could be described as known, familiar and relatively stable environments. The institutions we attend have the task to take care of all practical, logistical and organisational matters and provide for us a surprise-free, and hopefully enjoyable, space to focus on learning and developing into young adults. In normal circumstances, all we have to do is learn and mainly focus on our own achievements, developments and preparation for active adulthood, whilst others take care of us and provide for our needs.

But once we step into the world of work and join businesses of various sizes and structures, things changed dramatically and are turned almost upside down, even if the time elapsed between the previous familiar world and the new world of work is only that of a few weeks or months.

In the new world of work, we have responsibility, accountability and authority, and we cannot choose and have to work with those around us who often change and move in and out of our immediate circle of connections. We have to comply with demands from managers who we may not respect and deliver against set targets under risk of losing the income and the job. We now typically have financial responsibility for ourselves and often that of dependents and have to develop a new level of social and emotional intelligence to navigate politics and hierarchies and learn to manage perception, to name just a few of the new activities, skills and multiple roles that almost overnight we need to play and play well.

The world of work is a world where human nature is exposed, tested and forged in an environment that sometimes is nurturing and sometimes is toxic, with all shades in between.

Carefully considering, designing and maintaining the world of work and the organisational structures, functions and culture that hold it together and enable it to exist is a great responsibility that requires knowledge, careful thinking, empathy, art, science and technology, finely balanced and attuned to create the best experience and outcomes for the people at its centre.

Four reasons why design thinking is fit for purpose in the pursuit of adaptive digital organisations

In modern days, science is busy gathering a body of knowledge by use of scientific research methods as conducted in academic and research structures, whilst art employs means that appeal to our senses, emotions, fantasy and sensibility to beauty to enhance our experience of life in ways that imitate more or less reality, whilst stimulating imagination to nurture and sooth our spirit through storytelling and meaning making.

Beyond this duality sits the third way of the design thinking. It aims to find answers to existing real needs and problems by looking for solutions – like science does – but also to get inside the minds of those who will benefit from the design solutions and understand their subjective world of stories, expectations, motivations, feelings, emotions, beliefs and values – like art does – with the purpose to truly solve the problem or fully utilise an opportunity for something better, through the eyes of those who have put their hopes in the hands of solution designers.

Resting on principles that integrate humanity, change and outcomes

The unfolding of our lives follows a pattern that involves periods of stability and periods of great change. And there are moments recognised as critical transitions from one state to another in our personal lives such as leaving home to live by oneself, establishing lasting relationships with partners, having a family, moving from childhood to adulthood and adjusting to the process of aging. Other significant transitions relate to our cognitive development by way of knowledge and skills, through institutions such as preschool, school and technical colleges or higher education. All these stages prepare us for an independent and meaningful life of responsibility and contributions to others and for personal fulfilment and actualisation of our potential and dreams.

In one way of another, there is also an expectation of us to change, adapt and deliver something in exchange for what we receive from others and society, particularly when we join the world of work.

Whilst we do not change much and possibly not at all during the very short time that lapses between a life of study to a life of work, we are expected to step into a world which is pretty much upside down from what we knew, instantly adapt and hit the ground running. This is a new contract in which outcomes are the measure of our job security, and remuneration is based on professional performance. Having been students only weeks ago, we now have to act as masters of our skills and perform to commercial imperatives even when we don't yet understand that well what they are.

This dramatic change turns us from curious, alert, carefree, confident and effective individuals into utterly incompetent graduates, new entrants into the workforce who do not understand much about the world we find ourselves in. We find ourselves in an environment where every person we meet is new and seems to know what they are doing, where we may like or dislike the people we have to work with but have to work with them anyway, and where we may have to – for some time – keep asking questions and asking for help from colleagues even if we hate doing so because they are all very busy with their own work.

Gone are the certificates and the prizes we won during our school and university years, gone is our status of leaders in various interest groups and activities, gone is our reputation of high performance in sports or theatrical productions, gone are the high marks and praises received for essays and dissertations. We become the young new recruit who needs constant looking after because we have very little competence to actually deliver a good job from day one, and it will take months for us to come up to speed and be able to actually assess whether this job is what we really wanted to do or not.

But this is just one change – albeit in a class of its own – that we will experience in our working life. In a digital age, this is set to be much more dynamic and filled with opportunities, threats of great fragmentation, the need for reinvention and requirements for continuous learning and up-skilling. This will place demands on our adaptability and great reliance on our flexibility, agility and resilience to survive and hopefully thrive in this volatile environment.

We may find ourselves in offices that are not very well equipped, without access to information and systems necessary for our immediate activity. We are introduced to structures and hierarchies that we need to understand and work with whether we like it or not. We have to establish ourselves, build trust and credibility with everyone around us, learning as fast as we can, and hope that people around us will not be too critical, disappointed or doubtful about our performance.

The world of enterprise and business is a world where we do not get to choose who we work for or who our bosses and colleagues are. Often as soon as we establish connections and relationships that we value, we may see them move on and leave the organisation or go to other departments.

Change and outcomes are now necessary and scrutinised aspects of our new everyday working lives. All these demands on our performance make catering to humanity a necessary part of the process of being in work. The expectation is the design of work-related environments to support human beings and respect their feelings, personalities, skills and motivations and the demands that adaptation places on them. Designing for people should enable them to flourish in the long run, feel safe and secure and be happy to contribute to the enterprise agenda, their professional community and society at large.

Embracing solution-focussed divergent thinking and
multidisciplinary knowledge to be successful
in complex, dynamic and ambiguous contexts

Our world today is on the cusp of the Fourth Industrial Revolution, which brings with it significant changes. These are changes in terms of skills, professions, business management principles and individual traits and characteristics that appear imperative for a world that brings in AI and robotics as equal partners in our working and everyday lives.

In business and work, our task and obligation are to work within the environments and the people around us as they are, flexibly adapt and be able to make a contribution. Our work is supervised, sometimes by people we dislike or do not get along with or do not even respect. But our job requires us to get along because we get remunerated by the organisation against our performance, and therefore we need them as much as they need us.

This complex layering of factors at play that are dynamically co-dependent creates a world that is constantly changing, constantly reinventing itself and constantly challenging for those who operate within it. This is a world made of many facets, each quite different from the other, which nonetheless, somehow miraculously, come together to produce outcomes that are often quite extraordinary and account for humankind's progress over millennia such as the great achievements of technology, engineering and medicine.

In many ways, this is a demanding environment where people just need to get on and be at their best regardless of what comes their way, planned or unplanned, announced or unannounced. In some respects, this volatile and unpredictable system of changes can be invigorating for those who like change, are flexible and adapt quickly, swiftly establish rapport with others and effectively chart a professional path for themselves.

In this light, it is clear that a different way of thinking is required that engages higher thinking capabilities, solves complex problems, pays attention to relationships and collaboration, is able to make sense of things and define purpose, embraces science and technology, and develops cross-functional multidisciplinary thinking in our approach to life and work. This is particularly important when engaged in skilled activities such as setting up and managing businesses large and small in a world that is volatile, competitive and uncertain.

Success in these circumstances requires a different sustained attention span, ability to analyse as well as synthesise, capability to look ahead and watch for threats and opportunities, flexibility, agility and leadership. Such skills, competencies and capabilities are not easily acquired, nurtured or developed by fast, narrow and easy steps. There is no silver bullet that fits all needs and can get results on the spot. All these are complex capabilities that pull resources across hard and soft skills and combine them in supple and appropriate ways to circumstances, using convergent and divergent thinking, solution focus and a mixed body of knowledge from diverse teams and skills that come together to find answers to complex problems and challenges.

Dealing with "wicked problems" that are ill defined
in nature, from outset to outcome

People are the real source of all achievements and – paradoxically – also the source of all challenges, and if only we could discover and understand all that we can about people and work effectively with that knowledge, there would be no problems for us to solve other than those presented to us by nature. But people present an intriguing juxtaposition of traits and attributes that contradict each other and together cover the entire range of a continuum from incomprehensible evil and destruction to exceptional kindness and achievement.

Human beings like to criticise and praise, enjoy a fight as much as working together, like to collaborate but also to be led by a strong hand, enjoy peace alongside a long protracted war, risk their own lives and mend broken bodies as much as torture and dismember, are caring and kind to their young but also sell them for money and treat them as slaves, respect and care for the old, as well as neglect and abandon them. This is why when thinking about human beings, it is necessary to use a convergent and divergent thinking. On the one hand, we need to pay attention to specific disciplines for their in-depth level of information; on the other, we need to integrate a range of disciplines together, to better mirror reality and the interconnected way things pan out in actual life, to advance out full better understanding of the human condition.

Understanding human beings requires an integration of natural science, social science, art and technology to match the human nature. Human nature embodies cognition and abstractions, emotions and mood, creativity, innovation and technology, all converging to change and improve our experience of life, satisfy needs and solve problems that we face in the mixed environment presented by nature and created by human civilisation.

This approach re-creates a boundless explanatory complex and evolving system in which various forces are at work in ways that may

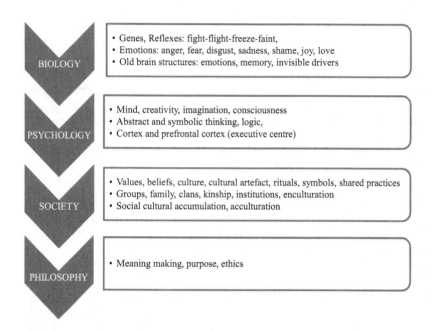

Figure 2.1 Complexity of human identity

be visible and subject to linear causality but also ways that are invisible and subject to unintended and hidden connections.

The impact and contribution of people to business and organisation success has long been established. However, how to make the best use of this collective capability remains, it seems, an art. Science and practice are still offering incomplete answers, although they both provide quite a solid platform of hypotheses and principles that could be better used to enhance our capability to work with people, through people and for the benefit of people. In business settings, people include both customers and those working in businesses and delivery.

The list of polarised capabilities in human behaviour is long and unsettling, and it is interesting to note that of the seven primary emotions that humans experience, love and joy are the only two positive ones; the rest are negative emotions such as anger, fear, shame and disgust.

Wisdom also argues that joy and love conquer and overpower everything else, and judging by the exceptional achievements that humans are capable of, most are imbued with positive emotions, feelings and aspirations that testify to their exceptional motivational power.

In addition, human beings are able make decisions governed by reason and informed by ethics, and this combined with consciousness creates another level of capability that is unique to our species and makes us so different and able.

But the "wicked nature" of understanding human motivations and human behaviour and the challenge around enabling full potential in life and work remain moving targets that cannot be followed by binary thinking and mechanistic causality. Instead, a sophisticated interrogative, third option that embraces complexity and multiple sources of knowledge combined may best suit the puzzle of human nature, in which neither the inputs not the outputs are clear, linear or well defined.

Working with virtual options as something that may become actual

The "hypothetical" activity that the human brain is capable of uses our capacity for abstract thinking, language and symbolic conversion of reality into a virtual facsimile held by our imagination. This activity is also required when we conceive of a business and design a future potential organisation.

Small businesses start with a person or a small number of people generating an idea about something that they think the market would need or want. The first step is to really define what that process or product is going to be, who is going to buy it and what it's going to look like.

The next step is to turn the idea into a prototype of service or product that moves the idea from a hypothesis to an actual outcome that can be tested on a small number of people to get feedback on likes or dislikes and identify improvements determined by fitness for purpose.

What follows is a succession of reviews of the prototype itself and iterations of test, re-design, re-test and so on, as a result of user, client or beneficiary feedback, to enable modifications and adaptations necessary to meet the needs identified by feedback loops.

Wide release and a sustained sales and marketing drive follow in the pursuit of financial returns. But often this drive meets the challenge of its own success because unless we envisage how to scale up the product or service availability and after-sales support, in the way customers expect to experience the end-to-end interaction with the enterprise, things can go terribly wrong. The problem of support at scale can happen at the very point of an apparent success of sales by failure in deliver to the customer's expectations created by the brand promise.

Operational capability has to be first envisioned and then implemented by a pool of specific skills and expertise. This needs an initial approach through hypothesis and abstract thinking in design and planning, working with concepts. Once the concept is established, then the ideas can become reality and can be refined by a feedback loop to a wider scope. These iterations that envision and realise repeatedly generate the grander and actual structures and functions of an enterprise.

This dynamic of design and realisation, in turn, is often sustained by other critical abstract considerations, namely, purpose, mission and vision – all of which are indeed ideas and inspirational drivers of something that does not exist as such but motivates and enables on the ground implementation, nonetheless. And this is how virtuality and actuality feeds back on each other.

Handshakes, interfaces and overlaps: a multidisciplinary and cross-functional perspective on applying knowledge to optimise business

Organisations are typically structured around functions and processes, and more often than not, one function is not necessarily aware of or respectful of the activities, value and importance of other functions. Known as "silos", some functions view themselves in isolation and as more important than others and so create an internal culture that lacks appreciation for what the other people in the company do.

The internal supply and value chain is not vertically and horizontally integrated, and contributors are not aware of the impact of good or poor quality and speed of execution of their specific outputs in the chain that exist to the left and the right of that specific process. In addition, people working in organisations tend to focus inwards and are not necessarily aware of their customers or their competitors out there in a dynamic global marketplace.

In reality, everything from staff to customers and back is interconnected. Engaged staff are more productive and interested in the quality of products and services that they deliver and the way their customers respond, who in turn would happily consume and endorse both the brand and the product and services that meet their expectations.

In this scenario, the feedback loops dynamically reinforce certain behaviours on both sides of the supply, value and consumption chain, with a positive outcome to those who have invested in such an enterprise. But this highlights the need for a way of working that is often challenging for most organisations, namely, working across boundaries of multidisciplinary bodies of knowledge and cross-functional domains. At the extreme, this extends into the opportunities and value chain created beyond the enterprise, in the market and society through customers and the role the enterprise itself plays in the greater good.

Mixed methodologies and teams can go a long way to eliminate divisions and create work and efficiency flows across internal and external boundaries.

Personally, I embrace a dialectics, dynamic and complex perspectives on business, society and the world – not least because such intricacy is evident even in what may be considered the most mechanistic settings, which upon scrutiny also extend beyond an easily established and tracked succession of linear sets of causality. But this is not about explaining my own position or persuading others to embrace it but rather providing some food for thought to those who would enjoy reflecting on how their own roles bring together interconnected aspects from a variety of sources.

Whilst we create and stay within artificial boundaries of specific focus, it is nonetheless obvious that the connections between various disciplines and functions go as far afield as we can imagine. Keeping in mind that the perspective we choose is just an artificial limitation to allow us to fully understand what we observe, it is useful to develop the curiosity and ability to mentally integrate the whole picture.

We also need to be aware that as long as we do not have a view of the entire picture, there is the risk of us missing out on active factors that could be critical to outcomes. Empathy and trying to see feel or do what others see, feel or do in their work can be very helpful. Design thinking upholds this principle and combined with complexity thinking forms a strong platform for us to improve our grasp on many factors that form the fabric of the organisation.

But whether we can at all times have complete knowledge and total grasp of reality in its entire complexity remains an open question on which both philosophy and science have different views.

Philosophy, ethics and critical business functions

Philosophy, including ethics, deals with the big questions about our lives, the way we have come to be and our role in the bigger scheme of things. Simple but profound questions such as "Who am I?" "Why am I here?" and "Where do I fit in the universe?" are fundamental to our human nature and our human desire to reflect and seek to make meaning and find purpose in our lives. As a branch of philosophy, ethics seeks answers to questions about morality, the right course of action to take in certain circumstances. Both theory and research in ethics have developed because of our natural ability as individuals and society to enquire about ourselves and our lives.

It is the same for the business environment where philosophy and ethics prevail, albeit expressed in different languages, through different organisation functions and as a result of different sets of business related activities. The financial crash of 2009 has been extremely damaging to many people on a global scale, and ten years later, the world has still not recovered from its consequences. The lack of trust in financial institutions followed by a general lack of trust in institutions and establishment in general have increased significantly to the point where there is a demand for attention and focus to be given by establishments to fundamental questions of ethics, responsibility to individuals, society and the environment and our legacy to future generations.

This reassessment of business goals is now questioning the "greed is good" mantra of the 1980s, the obsession with "shareholder return" of the 1990s or the astronomic rise in pay for CEOs as the rock stars and wonder children of globalised corporate world, now all under review in light of a reform needed in the practice of business philosophy and ethics.

By 2015, the tide changed, and today we are witnessing a new focus on the need for organisations to define for themselves – before mission, vision and objectives – their purpose of being. This is indeed a question of philosophical magnitude because it requires the business leadership to think beyond the bottom line of profit and loss and take a view on the role and responsibility of business in the global context of today and tomorrow.

In organisations, it is the leadership and management functions, the organisational culture and the human resources function that together are responsible for translating philosophical and ethical considerations into purpose, mission, vision, values, beliefs and strategic business objectives, all the way down to setting individual business objectives for all the people involved in the organisation.

The creation of business purpose is realised in through mechanisms such as performance management, internal communication, internal organisational structure, roles and responsibilities, and quality management. Business culture demonstrates not only the connection between philosophy and ethics and the workings of an organisation but also the interconnection between various aspects of internal organisational function that together bring to life the abstract thinking that sits at the top of the business hierarchy and work together as interrelated forces.

Technology, computer science, artificial intelligence and ethics

Ever since the information technology revolution of 1969, the world has been pretty much run by computer science. The rise of computer technology has enabled the creation of relevant infrastructure and software, leading to applications such as the smart phone, computers, the Internet, automation and robotics and technological platforms for social media and e-commerce. All these innovations burst into being and clustered around the 1980s, rapidly evolving into what we today call the cusp of the fourth digital revolution. Software applications that are present pretty much in every home and literally in the hands of almost every person on the planet have also revealed the dual aspects of human nature – generosity and selfishness, empathy and cruelty, creativity and destruction, harm and healing, all exercised on the dark or bright web – and have raised ethical questions around the way applied science and technology challenge our values, beliefs and thoughts on what is right and what is wrong, linking us back to philosophy and ethics.

Democratised technology is also straining our control of how can we practically resolve such deep concerns about internet threats to individual wellbeing and life (self-harm, suicide, trolls and so on) or matters of privacy for millions whose data have been captured and stored or threats to free choice and manipulation of the democratic processes in elections, when it comes to application of existing and clearly inadequate regulatory mechanisms that govern the activities of global technology providers. The harvesting, storage and use of data that businesses hold on their customers and suppliers and their own employees – for example – has been raising questions about business policies in relation to our privacy and confidentiality as well as protection of data from cyberattacks and misuse.

Businesses such as financial institutions, social media platforms, providers of software linked to the Internet Of Things and national health organisations have all been forced to push ethical considerations around their obligations, all the way up to the highest level of decision making within the organisation leadership. At the same time, these organisations are dealing with increased regulatory activity by governments. Again, this is a case of business practice across many interrelated functions of the organisation that are forced to refer back to questions of a fundamental and apparently theoretical nature around philosophy and ethics.

The result of abstract and applied thinking generates feedback loops between science and practice, between theory and reality in an ongoing process of review that has seen, and is likely to continue to see, the business activity reflecting new thought and trends in scientific thinking. The recent developments in AI and robotics and the significant impact that they will have on the future of work, professions, generation of wealth, potential social divisions, changes in social structures and changes in skills and business processes have thankfully triggered an increased interest in our considerations about what we really know about human nature as well as the ethical implications of potential human machine collaborations.

Dreams of technology have triggered both utopian and dystopian visions for the future of humanity impacted by the unprecedented changes brought about by this latest digital revolution. The lag between applied technology and ethical consideration has been shortened by a spreading concern for ethical and regulatory reflections and a desire for measures to swiftly follow if not coincide with the fast technological pace.

This desire for ethical measures has grown so much so that ethics forums and committees are being set up within business and society, not only locally or within companies but also as global alliances designed to influence policy and actual business practice and organisational behaviour, culture and leadership from the top down. Such structures are typically cross-disciplinary and multifunctional in nature, whether set at the individual business or global level and all the levels between.

Dialectics, complexity theory, supply chain and project management

Dialectic philosophy posits that reality exists as a dynamic complex changing and evolving state in which with the passing of time, there are transformation and renewal, in which the seeds of the future are sown in the past, in which things constantly evolve in increasingly sophisticated states of being as the internal antagonistic forces of renewal manifest themselves.

Its corollary in science is represented by the complex evolving systems theory, which defines and describes ten key principles – out of many – that operate in complex adaptive systems: feedback, connectivity, interdependence, emergence, far from equilibrium, space of possibilities, co-evolution, historicity and time, path dependence and creation of new order.

The complexity theory in science upholds the view of dynamic and evolving transformation of complex systems, with human systems, society and organisations as examples of such complex adaptive systems. Specific business activities such as manufacturing and supply chain are "business as usual" examples of interdependent systems of exceptional intricacy and complexity, and I cannot imagine anything more complex than manufacturing and supply chain activities that link processes, people, products, services, customers, natural resources, environmental impact, financial systems and ecology so organically and so unequivocally.

There are entire organisational processes, practices, sets of skills, human resources, quality systems, compliance controls, regulation and legislation, purpose and ethics, technology and finance that are all interconnected and all driving forward the transformation of an intention into an actual outcome. In this interrelated and interconnected web of organisational functions, the principles at work very much reflect the principles stated by the complex evolving systems theory. The modern supply chain indeed operates with methodology and applications that are designed to take the pulse of every step in the process and adjust the rest of the system to handle intended or unintended variations that always occur in networks of such magnitude.

The reality of business today is that it has become more vulnerable not only to its own internal pressures, many brought in by new generational expectations, but also to changes in the wider environment as they occur through various players in the vastness of the global system. The outside world itself is increasingly ambiguous, volatile and uncertain; general or specific information inputs – used to determine the enterprise's direction of travel – can change unexpectedly or can be unclear from the outset and lead to unexpected outcomes.

As a result, even the methodology of project management – an orderly way whereby specific objectives are made tangible and achieved – has to take into account unpredictability and variability. The great success of the agile methodologies in project management since the early 2000, as well as the extension of the agile philosophy and practice into other aspects of overall business and organisation development (O/D) are clear adaptive testimonials of how important complexity thinking has become as the guiding philosophy for practice in science and business.

Neuroscience, sociology, employee and customer engagement and gamification

Neuroscience is part of medicine and specifically focusses on the activity of the nervous system and the brain. Knowledge about the brain structure and the various formations within the brain has existed for a very long time. Alongside this knowledge have been assumptions and verified understanding of how various parts of the brain work and what kind of responsibilities they have for different activities. Together all parts of the brain give rise to our consciousness and our psyche. But neuroscience has moved forward in leaps and bounds since the 1980s, and technology has enabled visualisation of the brain's activity in real time and in vivo.

Interestingly, a lot of the previous assumptions and knowledge that has been gathered, despite the unsophisticated methods used, have held their value. In addition, a lot of other functionalities of the brain, the relationships between the various activities in different parts of the brain and the activity at the microscopic levels of the neuron and the neuronal networks, have provided exciting and to a degree, view changing information.

Since the 1800s, psychologists, psychiatrists and therapists have been mentioning, in a scientific context, assumptions about the subconscious and unconscious activities of the mind, alongside the rational conscious contribution that the cortex, which is the thinnest and most newly developed part of the brain, offers us.

Today we can actually see the regions of the brain responsible for conscious and subconscious activity in action, and we have increasingly had to pay attention to the fact that many of our decisions and triggers of behaviour do not actually reside in our rational brain but are instead driven by the older and more primitive parts of the brain that have historically been responsible for keeping us alive. In addition, our knowledge of the biochemistry of the brain, including various hormones and biochemical processes that happen alongside the electrical activity of the brain, is also increasing our understanding of the hidden workings of our mind.

This integrated appreciation of the functioning brain has given rise to a degree of enthusiasm for more knowledge and education around the hidden processes that are the root of our visible reactions and behaviours, including the functional and helpful ones as well as the ones that act as blockers to our best intentions.

The link between the science of the brain and its workings and the individual and collective behavioural consequences that manifest in organisations, at an individual, team or organisation-wide level are of consequence when it comes to developing leadership and management capabilities. This link is also important to establishing and utilising organisational culture, values and beliefs and the overall effectiveness of an organisation as the engine of achieving business objectives.

Education processes, training and development programs have been galvanised through the appreciation of subconscious and unconscious processes. These processes are located around the middle of the brain in structures such as the limbic system, amygdale and hypothalamus; they are responsible for the primary emotions of anger, sadness, disgust, fear, shame, joy and love, alongside the release of mood-related hormones, and the activity of reflex actions of fight flight, freeze and faint.

Training programs, alongside coaching and self-development programs for management and leadership, form part of the quest for improvement of individual and collective behaviour in organisations. These programs enhance people's awareness of the counterproductive and potential dark side of the brain's biology. This training focusses on the more socialised and collaborative capabilities of individuals acting as part of social groups, particularly in business settings.

The knowledge about the unconscious activity of the brain and its response to external stimuli has also enhanced the creation of communication and manipulation mechanisms already used in marketing since the 1950s. Marketing and advertising use techniques to stimulate and trigger reactions through unconscious processes, used in e-commerce to create and enhance for example customer experience. But nudging behavioural reactions or unconscious biases or emotions is also a way to increase employee engagement. The same mechanisms can be used to appeal to the unconscious and conscious mind and align individuals to a desired behaviour or culture displayed by a group, resulting in collaboration and cohesions within others.

As a result, internal and external advertising and a host of new approaches to branding, engagement and behavioural change – as used, for example, in gamification – have been increasingly rolled out with great enthusiasm. The hope that these new techniques will be the silver bullet – which they are not – may be misplaced but using them as a purposely designed method in the mix, to be deployed for specific business outcomes, can certainly add another technology enabled way to optimise enterprises. In addition, gamification uses design thinking, another new discipline refined at the turn of the millennium, which itself is based on empathy and the ability to appreciate the deeper connections to the beneficiary's unconscious needs dreams and desires. But both design thinking and gamification use the sciences of psychology, sociology, anthropology and evolutionary and behavioural psychology to work with the powerful forces that naturally manifest in individuals and groups and use that energy to modify behaviours towards positive business related outcomes.

Today the enablement of social media through technological platforms has proven how much public opinion can influence the reputation and success of businesses. Social media influences the way businesses are perceived and evaluated en masse, through social memes, fashions, fads and all the forces of group dynamics, such as roles, status, competition, fellowship and leadership, that are at work in our human societies.

Both those who create products and those who buy them are human beings subject to the same bio-psycho-sociological forces that end up translated in behaviours. And the interest demonstrated by business in the findings of the newer kid on the block of knowledge – neuroscience – is telling of the appetite that exists for gaining a deeper understanding of people, particularly when driven by invisible underlying forces that act beneath the tangible and impact outcomes in business and society.

We also accept today that whilst we may not have all the answers about everything, aspects of reality that may be ill defined exist nonetheless and may exercise their influence in ways that are also often difficult to predict. In this regard, neuroscience, complexity thinking, dialectic philosophy and social and behavioural sciences are all shaking hands in an attempt to offer a holistic and integrated view of human nature and by extension how we can apply that knowledge and what we may hope to achieve towards increasing organisation effectiveness.

Quality, standards, social sciences and business

The evolution of quality thinking and practice has moved from quality assurance, to quality management, to total quality management focussing in the process on inspection of finished products, then to the design of the process for the production of the defect free outputs, and finally to include the entire supply and value chain around products. The general perception of quality management in business is about metrics, controls, precision and a degree of repetition and rigid processing. Why this is the case remains a question to be answered because in fact the philosophy of the quality founding fathers and early contributors couldn't stand further from this view. They emphasised the critical importance of the "soft" aspects of quality and revolved mainly around people's contribution and potential and the compelling necessity to create an organisational climate and culture that enables the manifestation of this potentially untapped and often poorly managed treasure.

In their philosophy, the key founders of modern (1940s–1970s) quality management (Deming and Ishikawa creator of the Toyota Production System) placed great importance on treating employees with respect, enabling them to have a voice and contribute to improvements and solution generation, fostering a climate of openness and valued collective contributions and appreciating individual inputs regardless of status and ranks. In their vision, engaging employees means breaking down the barriers between management and staff, engaging people through pride of achievement, recognition of contributions, eliminating internal silos and fostering a culture of improvement at micro and macro levels. And desired quality can be achieved by small incremental positive changes in known established processes or radical transformations of process through new thinking and technology that come together in innovation.

Personally, I am struck by the similarities between the fashionable agile methodology and the less glamorous quality methodology. Having said that, there are quality standards and quality awards that clearly state, in formal principles, standards and requirements, the exceptional focus that they have on employees, management practices and the value of relationships across the entire human chain involved in business – end to end – from suppliers to customers.

Quality thinking is a philosophical thinking because it really sets standards and aspirations that carry through the entire business activity. It is attached to people, who are the very lifeline of business. In so doing, quality involves other sciences such as psychology, neuroscience, anthropology and sociology because it deals with values and beliefs, aspirations and the deeper subjective drivers of our human nature.

In modern business language, whether we talk about the customer experience and employee experience, about value for money in products and services or about sustainability, legacy and our responsibility for current and future generations, we always talk about something that we wish to achieve and do so to a certain high standard.

In one word, we always talk about quality when we mention something that is good. The keywords in Deming's manifesto or the "Toyota Way" could not be closer to the agile manifesto, around the value of people and collaborations. Past and present aspirations of achievement reflect our contemporary challenges, albeit expressed in language that, as all things linked to society, evolves to use new but also pre-existing meanings and needs. What is different is the way we fulfil them now as opposed to then through solutions that reflect the taste and expectations of our times.

Neuroscience, marketing and ethics

Born around the 1950s, marketing was the first commercially focussed approach to use psychology in business to augment consumer product sales in the booming post–World War 2 economy of the USA. Already enabled by the industrial revolutions of 1784 and 1890, manufacturing had made huge leaps of productivity through mechanised and electrified means of production that were churning household goods, heralding a new era of domestic comfort and luxury. And marketing (supported by consumer psychology) became the applied science and business function that was able to move these products on, to consumers convinced to purchase what they needed but also enticed to acquire what they did not need at all but were made to very much desire and aspire to own.

To this day, marketing uses unconscious manipulation of emotions that human beings experience, particularly around anxiety and desires. Cleverly captured and packaged in words and imagery, they trigger subliminal and symbolic connotations to enviable lifestyles symbolised by objects that – post-acquisition – promise to become magic portals and transport the consumers to another, much better experience, over and beyond their modest station and ordinary life or to avoid some social stigma.

The aspiration to be someone else, be better off, or at least join as a peer – if not surpass – those whose growing wealth is increasingly flaunted, is based on envy, desire, fantasy and magical thinking, all well-known mechanisms of the psyche linked to our primitive brain and the imagination that children use in play, when they place themselves in roles and situations that do not exist except in their mind but helped in reality by token objects that symbolise such imaginary worlds. In the case of marketing, this relates to ordinary people imagining that they have accessed and share in the world of their idols – celebrities, stars, VIPs – by proxy and by use of similar or same objects as they do.

Today this manipulation of the mainly unconscious emotions of desire, anxiety, envy and narcissism has reached global proportions enabled by social media and the long list of reality TV programs that keep the watchful eye of the camera on the most intimate details of the "rich and famous" day in day out. This coverage is endless, with similar franchises of the same type gone global. Everyone can see how the other 1% live whilst purchasing, consuming, imitating and aspiring to become like them, when – in fact – staying where we are in most cases. The aspiration to become a celebrity and very rich, very fast is now one of the newest and accepted aspirations of the children of social media, and all manner of reality TV contests and games promise a fast track to that coveted place.

Whilst a lot of ethical questions can be asked, what remains a fact is that such a use of the psychology of our primitive brain and unconscious processes works and captures the imagination of the masses. A job well done by marketing in the service of conspicuous consumption to achieve profit by all means.

Gamification has also been on the rise since 2000. It and has achieved its objectives of engaging people and facilitating changes to behaviour by using psychology and the fundamental aspects that define generally human behaviour, human motivation and human responses to stimulation. Again, the bad comes packaged with the good, and questions have been raised about non-coercive influence and manipulation, addiction, lack of intrinsic motivators and band-aid applicability.

Putting such considerations aside, this is another example of how different disciplines and functions come together, bringing in this case, psychology, art, technology, e-commerce, manufacturing and supply chain into an integrated body that is together utilised in business and life.

Organisation development, agile and complexity theory

The intention of making organisations more productive and ensuring organisational functionality, development and effectiveness has been well served since the 1930s by exceptionally capable thinkers and practitioners who have put forward models, methodologies and tools to guide us.

Such contributions have reflected the flavour of the times and have also evolved with the philosophical and scientific thinking of the times. In fact, everything that has been historically produced in this regard still holds its value depending on the context and specifics of the business itself and its wider environment. It is also true that different tools and models are applicable to different business functions or even specific teams and leadership types or cultures.

But the changes that have happened in the wider global system have brought uncertainty, volatility and ambiguity to business activity, as well as technology that has provided enormous opportunities for business streamlining and automation have all changed the landscape of business operations today.

Changes to business include the size and make-up of companies and the type of products and services they deliver, all of which are pretty much enabled by information technology, communication and digitally integrated systems that serve business processes and people in their daily tasks. In the light of extreme unprecedented transformation of the internal landscape of business, the thinking and theory of O/D have also evolved to bring into consideration dialectics and complex evolving systems theory as a more appropriate perspective than a mechanistic rigid view of the world.

In this light, new classifications of organisations have been produced that reflect the acceptance that change and development of structures can be impacted by external or internal forces in unpredictable ways and require the development of capabilities that enable agility, flexibility and resilience in the face of change. As a result, many operating principles of complex evolving systems theory have been embraced as part of the organisational development theory with the entire organisational system also being considered as potentially operating on the edge of chaos.

This realisation pushes the boundaries of adaptation demands an organisational system to work towards finding a new equilibrium and abandon its previous state of balance if it is to survive and continue on, albeit under a different guise. Organisations are not only part of chains of events that extend way beyond their own boundaries but are also subject to the dynamic exchanges that happen internally between the various business functions and the way they coordinate, adjust and collaborate in the successful pursuit of a unified purpose and a set of objectives.

Whilst earlier thinking around organisations connected to a more mechanistic view of the world, in which precise scientific control and firm linear causality were used as rational guidelines to success, today it is accepted that probability and chance also play roles and that in complex dynamic systems, change cannot be planned and controlled but rather enabled. Such theoretical thinking has given rise to new models of O/D in which flexible factors, such as servant leadership or enabling leadership, for example, are engines of change in uncharted waters.

Equally, distributed leadership, collaboration and collective contribution and cross-functional agile project teams that have input into constant improvements and generate innovative solutions to challenges are increasingly becoming a model embraced by all organisations, including large corporations who foster pockets of agile activity within their wider and more stable structures.

The earlier examples are only a few of the many that can demonstrate the permutations and combination of disciplines and functions that are in fact interrelated in the dynamic world of life and work.

Acknowledging this awareness and embracing a flexible integrated view of multiple domains of activity and knowledge can only get us closer to understanding and working with reality in a harmonious, stimulating and effective way.

Dealing with change and the ongoing adaptive development of agile digital enterprises

Designing organisations and utilising multidisciplinary cross-functional sources of knowledge is not enough to ensure optimum organisational dynamics. The measure of success is in the way the enterprise works in pursuit of its purpose and how well it implements its processes, technology and policies by changing in agile and flexible ways.

Organisation development is a vast field of theory, research and practice that serves precisely the purpose to enable and maintain the more effective and successful organisational change programs that are rolled out to support adaptation necessary to respond to change internal and external factors and continue to dynamically pursue objectives.

Organisation development has enjoyed many decades of attention and accumulated a multitude of theoretical frameworks and models and a strong grounding for the development of change practice methodology. Change process research and implementation research occupy relatively separate intellectual spheres, a divide not uncommon between academia and practice. This divide typically hinders further development regarding organisations and change, due partly to unavoidable limitations of domain specific methodologies and integrating findings and value offered by each. Combining the findings of research and implementation is the ideal way to get the best of the significant advances accumulated so far.

Broadly speaking, O/D covers subfields such as O/D theory, O/D change theory and O/D implementation and practice.

Organisation development is interdisciplinary in nature and combines theory of personality and motivation. O/D also includes industrial and organisational psychology in addition to sociology and general psychology, so the foundation of this field of applied science rests with behavioural science. However, in recent times, expertise coming from systems thinking and organisational learning as well as coaching mentoring have added an increased multidisciplinary and interdisciplinary approach to O/D.

Organisation development rests on humanistic values such as:

- Considering people as human beings and not just resources for organisational productivity
- Enabling individual and organisational full potential
- Aiming to achieve all set organisational goals
- Creating a stimulating and exciting environment for the work
- Enabling people in the organisation to have a voice and impacted the way they relate to the organisation, their work and the wider environment
- Treating each person as an individual with their own complex identity and needs that are important for their work and life

The use of such humanistic values in organisations aims to enable the objectives of O/D that are to:

- Align employees' vision with that of the organisation.
- Increase interpersonal trust and create a culture which encourages individual participation and enthusiasm.
- Effectively manage conflict and encourage people to confront and solve problems rather than avoid them.
- Increase levels of collaboration, communication and success in achieving common objectives.
- Increase the ability to manage conflict and levels of employee satisfaction.
- Design and implement processes that help the operations of the organisation on a continuous basis.
- Replace hierarchies and levels of authority with the valuing of contributions of skill and knowledge.
- Prepare employees for change and develop their ability to break stereotypes.
- Enable managers with management techniques that can introduce change systematically, leading to greater organisational effectiveness.

In the 1940s and 1950s significant contributions to classical organisation theories have been made by Weber, Taylor and Fayol.

Weber's theory posits the organisation as a formal structure and a segment of the wider society. It is based on the five principles of: structure, specialisation, predictability and stability, rationality and democracy.

Taylor's approach is based on planning for efficiency, specialisation, standardisation and simplification.

Fayol's theory, known as the administrative theory, relates to management responsibility for planning, organising, training, commanding and coordinating by detailed functions such as division of work, authority and responsibility, discipline, unity of command, unity of direction, subordination of individual interest to general interest, remuneration of personnel, centralisation, scalar chain, order, equity, stability of tenure of personnel, initiative, esprit de corps, the concept of line and staff and committees.

For more than five decades, a rich range of theories and models have been developed for organisational diagnosis and change many based on the more modern ideas of open system theory based on Von Bertalaffy's thinking. Post 2008 fresh contributions have been made to theories that look at the relationship between organisations and their environment as well as their ability to adapt to environmental changes, introducing Falletta's organisational intelligence model and the Semantic Network Analysis from Zarei, Chaghouee and Ghapanchi. Such examples are:

1 Force field analysis (1951)
2 Leavitt's model (1965)
3 Likert system analysis (1967)
4 Weisbord's six-box model; (1976) defined by focussing on one major output, exploring the extent to which consumers of the output are satisfied with it and tracing the reasons for any dissatisfaction
5 Congruence model for organisation analysis (1977)
6 Mckinsey 7s framework (1981–1982)
7 Tichy's technical political cultural (TPC) framework (1983)
8 High-performance programming (1984)
9 Diagnosing individual and group behaviour (1987)
10 Burke-Litwin model of organisational performance and change (1992)

The Burke-Litwin (Warner Burke and George Litwin) Model is still widely used and helps O/D practitioners define areas of first- and second-order change. It has become the foundation of what is now known as transactional and transformational leadership, applied in leadership development as an O/D intervention.

The complexity theory and change

Complexity theory, initially known in natural science, mathematics and computer algorithms, has an application in O/D in regards to the emergence of order and structure in chaotic and complex organisational systems.

Beginning with the 1990s, a number of contributors such as Wheatley, Morgan, Black and Stacey challenge the idea of orderly business-as-usual change in organisations and instead theorise a view of business as a non-linear system where change cannot really be managed but instead is supported by leaders, who allow individuals to adapt whilst the organisation self-manages and moves to the edge of chaos.

This reflects complexity theory, which posits that some systems are chaotic in nature and can change significantly because of minor inputs, so these systems cannot be fully known in their entirety and with certainty. Learning to navigate change by adapting and flexing are the real ways to ensure organisational effectiveness.

There is a fine balance to be struck between too much stability, leading to stagnation and lack of proactive adaptation, and too little stability that renders the organisation unmanageable.

There are several stage based models of change in O/D that provide a systematic overview of the developmental potential of organisations, for example:

- Ken Wilber's integral theory
- William Torbert's action inquiry model
- Don Beck and Chris Cowan's spiral dynamics model
- Richard Barrett's corporate transformation model

Organisation development implementation and practice

The action aspect of O/D is realised by learning processes known as interventions. These are structured activities that involve the members of the client system and are introduced either by an external or internal change agent. Structured activities include questionnaires, interviews, group discussions, experiential exercises and attitude surveys.

An intervention can be considered to be any action that influences an organisation's improvement program in a change agent–client system relationship.

In O/D, the basic units of change are teams or groups and not individuals, a perspective which informs the following approaches:

1 One goal must be that of reducing competition and establishing internal collaboration.
2 Other general goals are to develop trust in communication and confidence across and between all levels.
3 Decision making resides with knowledge and information and is not located with hierarchy or role.
4 Management against achievements of goals sits with subunits and individuals, whilst controls are only interim measurements and enablers and not part of management strategy.
5 Only if people affected by change are allowed to participate, own, plan and conduct change will they really support it.

Interventions range from improving effectiveness of individuals to that of teams and groups. Interventions also impact effectiveness of relationships and integration throughout the organisation. Interventions may focus on task, or process or the mechanism they emphasise (e.g. education, interaction, conflict, communication, skill, practice, awareness, cultural norms). Such interventions are often led by change agents.

A change agent in O/D is a person who has knowledge of social sciences and human behaviour alongside training in intervention techniques who enables the people in a changing organisation to solve their problems and achieve their goals. Change agents can be internal or external; for example, an internal agent can be a member of staff who has the relevant capability as defined earlier. A change agent can be chosen either because of their prior qualification or because they have been trained by a specialist in the knowledge and techniques that are needed.

In addition to implementing an intervention, the change agent also has the task of creating a safe and favourable climate for learning and change that, when enabled, take on a spiral form, cycling through the improvement process while striving upwards to new levels of performance. In an unsafe environment, learning does not flourish and may stop altogether. People do not disclose their feelings, do not benefit from feedback and do not experiment with new "risky" ways. Hierarchy, authority, span of control and specialisation inhibit experimentation.

Change agents may be inhibited by all of these factors but are helped by factors such as:

1   A real need for change
2   Real support from management
3   Working by example and demonstrating supporting behaviours
4   Knowledge of social and behavioural sciences and systems theory
5   A belief in the human nature as a capable and competent source to do things better

Examples of interventions:

• Team building
• Coaching
• Large group interventions
• Mentoring
• Feedback on performance and appraisals
• Restructuring and downsizing
• Total quality management (TQM)
• Leadership development

In addition, there are also change efforts such as:

1   Operation management
2   Training and development
3   Technological change and innovation

Change agents, sponsors, self-managing teams and systems

Ideally, leaders committed to "knowledge leadership" can be effective change agents in organisations. Such leaders can appropriate, translate or transpose knowledge to their own environment. Another necessary factor is the acceptance of the client organisation that there is a problem and to make a decision to identify and correct it. The essential nature of O/D is to create a "helping relationship" in which the change agent helps the organisation to identify and resolve their problem by using multidisciplinary knowledge from psychology, sociology, anthropology, behavioural economics, communication and business administration theory through action research. This involves preliminary diagnosis, data collection, feedback, data exploration, and action planning and action deployment.

Organisation development deals with the organisation as a system with subsystems or parts (groups, structures, norms, values, outputs) with interconnections to external environments. All elements are viewed as interdependent.

Organisation development also focusses on total culture and cultural processes within the organisation, with the group considered as the key influence on individuals and personalities.

One effective way to engage groups is to enable them to become "self-managing". This empowers the group to set, control, use feedback and decide everything about that group from who is hired, to how the workday is organised and how much people are paid.

Modern view of organisation development and the question of its sweet spot in the digital age

The tremendous changes experienced by our human civilisation in the decades following the 1980s have introduced new and significant forces that have changed the face of organisations. Change has been driven by the impact of technology; globalisation; geopolitical and economic power shifts; generational differences in values and beliefs; new attitudes, opportunities and behaviours in both clients and employees; the transformation of organisations from hierarchical and mechanistic to collaborative and flatter structured networks; new leadership styles; and new personal attributes and capabilities required of all those involved in business as well as an overall pressure to increase resilience and adaptability.

All these changes have, of course, also raised questions about how fit for purpose the thinking and practice of established O/D is for the world we live in and, more important, for the future world of organisations. As a result both, academics and practitioners are critiquing and questioning the existing approaches with a view to update and upgrade what we know worked in the past to something that we may need to redesign to work in the future.

In this light, O/D can be viewed as a transformative approach to align strategy and systems leading to a desired vision and outcome. O/D thrives in a culture of innovation and cultural awareness that is supported by a leadership that utilises the best that technology can offer.

The 21st century O/D has to be invigorated and regenerated in light of the fundamental impact caused by robotics, AI, genetics and biotechnology and their applications that demand careful integration of human and technological capabilities to achieve a positive outcome.

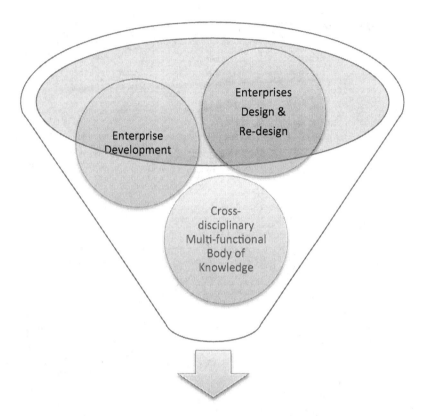

ENTERPRISE ADAPTATION

Figure 2.2 Dialectics and complexities of adaptive enterprise development

Organisation development has to play a part in serving the optimistic – not to say utopian – vision of the future and allay fears about doom and destruction. To achieve this, it is imperative that our perspective of organisations is holistic and integrative. We need to regard people in the context of their work in the wider environment and move away from simple causality and analysis of behaviour to introduce attention to emotions and human drivers such as values, beliefs and meaning.

We must identify challenges across the dynamic organisational system rather than in silos and that we embrace a cross-disciplinary perspective when bringing knowledge into O/D work and deploying it across-functions. O/D extends not only through the organisational network but also beyond, into the strengths and quality of relationships that the organisation has with its external systems.

Organisation development today and tomorrow will be about capability to integrate and take a holistic view of the business and world as interconnected and interdependent.

The agile enterprise

One example of a dynamic and integrated approach in practice is the agile enterprise, inspired by the software development methodology of the same name.

Agile software development methodology and principles have captured the zeitgeist of the decades after the turn of the 21st century, as the world has become an increasingly complex and volatile environment. The Agile method was developed to resolve issues of uncertainty, complexity and dynamic goals that the software development community was presented with in situations when the waterfall method of planned and linear execution of the project could not be used. The problem was due to lack of clarity of both the problem to be resolved as well as the desired solution and outcomes. The incomplete understanding of project components, their interactions or of changing requirements led to the setup of parallel work streams instead of sequential streams. In addition, the focus of the work effort morphed from detailed implementation of a succession of well-defined steps to setting goals achievable in every execution cycle. The succession of such successful cycles allows various options of the solution to emerge, whilst best choices are being made as work progresses.

Such principles translate in organisation dynamics and O/D approaches that display flexibility and speed of execution in potentially parallel streams (agile) whilst being driven in line with purpose, mission, vision and values towards swift implementation.

The combination of planning and execution allows organisations to look for the optimal path that will progressively clarify work tasks and adjustments and changes to requirements, trending towards the overall goal.

The agile enterprise aims to introduce change as a permanent element of organisational life and avoid the otherwise traumatic response that paralyses businesses when suddenly confronted with the necessity of change and the imperative of quickly adapting to new markets and environments.

By embracing change as a permanent force in organisation dynamics, the agile enterprise can actively take advantage of opportunities and deflect challenges.

The agile enterprise views itself as part of a wider system and acknowledges the interdependence among the various activities of systems, subsystems and ecosystems and the ripple effects that they may cause across the entire network.

Since the 1980s, the model of hierarchical complexity developed by Michael Lamport Commons (b. 1939, theoretical behavioural scientist and a complex systems scientist) and others has been used to describe stages of complexity in enterprise architecture. Enterprise architecture itself is a discipline that supports business agility through a variety of techniques such as separation of concerns; architecture framework; and separation of dynamics, stable components and layering.

Agility, for example, is supported by one type of enterprise architecture that is non-hierarchical. In this architecture, individuals function autonomously but maintain constant interaction r to define their aims and vision, maintain a shared understanding of requirements and monitor the work that needs to be done. Roles and responsibilities emerge from individuals' self-organising activities and are not set but remain in flux. Projects can be generated everywhere in the enterprise as well as from the outside. Interventions, intelligence, knowledge and power are distributed through the enterprise, and decisions are made by collaboration, on the fly and on the spot. This architecture makes the enterprise resilient and capable of quickly recovery and adaptation after the loss of any key enterprise component.

An agile enterprise clearly relates to complex systems science and principles such as:

Self-organisation: describing feedback driven exchanges that are spontaneous and not pre planned and which support important initiatives in the enterprise that are not initiated and managed by one person or party but emerges as a result of collective decision-making. This gives the organisation and edge when it comes to developing and redeveloping products and solutions for a market that is dynamic, highly competitive and changing.

Interactions are an important driving force in the agile enterprise because they represent exchanges between individuals who collectively hold behaviours, expertise, resources, competence and experience. The dynamic interactions give rise to new ideas for product services and solutions that emerge whilst exchanges continue to happen. It is the outcomes of these interactions that become drivers of change and innovation in agile enterprises.

Co-evolution is a result of the enterprise changing and constantly evolving as a result of and in relation to external factors via a process during which the enterprise learns from experience and adapts. Products and services are constantly challenged by competitors, regulators, suppliers and customers after they are launched and as a result of force adaptation. Co-evolution is the driver of constant review and refinement of the enterprise's outputs, in turn forcing it to adapt.

The edge of chaos represents the fine line between randomness and anarchy on the one hand and a state of equilibrium on the other. The tension between constant change and the forces that moderate the change energy (resistance to change, assumptions, need to recover and consolidate or a pre-existing state of equilibrium) keep the enterprise in a state of relative balance for a while, which also enables generation of new ideas and innovation. Self-organising and co-evolution flourish on the edge of chaos.

Today the techniques initially applied in software development have long crossed the boundaries into other mainstream activities industries such as the development of medical devices, motor vehicles, computers, music, clothing and food. Agile principles have also been applied in aspects of business management such as risk, finance, governance and strategy and are known as agile business management or business agility.

Business agility utilises agile techniques, principles, values and practices across the domains of:

• Integrated customer engagement involving customers in the delivery process to share accountability
• Facilitation-based management with the role being to facilitate the distributed ownership and completion of the day-to-day operations
• Adoption of incremental and iterative work practices across business functions from human resources, sales and marketing to finance (similar to scrum, Kanban, feature-driven development and test-driven development used in software)
• Promoting staff engagement and personal autonomy within an enabling organisational structure covered by outcomes
• Use of agile processes to business intelligence, big data, data science and data analytics (lean manufacturing, DevOps and DataOps)

Agile software development paradigms have also made it into mainstream lives and are used in household management or raising children by applying principles such as awareness, communication and adaptation.

Bibliography

Csíkszentmihályi, M. (1996). *Creativity: Flow and the psychology of discovery and invention.* New York: Harper Perennial.

Hegel, G. W. F. (1967). *Phenomenology of mind,* J. B. Baille (Trans.). London: Harper & Row.

Mitleton-Kelly, E. (1998). *Organisations as complex evolving systems.* LSE and Warwick Conference on Organisations as Complex Evolving Systems. Warwick, Dec. 4–5.

3 SOCIETALByDesign™ Model of adaptive enterprise design and development

When embracing what is good for society and planet means doing good business

The triad of logos, ethos and pathos is a reminder that our intelligence and logic, as used in technology and AI cannot be separated from our emotions and the ethics that surround how we use the applications that our extraordinary mind can create through its cognitive function.

Adina Tarry, *Coaching with Careers and AI in Mind*

My first visit to the USA in the 1980s took me to a country very different from the Europe at that time, and I found myself on the first day in one of the famous shopping malls which have sprung up there many years before this side of the pond – formidable citadels of consumption that took the economic optimism of the postwar American to a level of opulent consumerism that I had never seen before.

I was simply looking for a toothbrush and toothpaste, but I found myself in a maze of long alleys with countless shelves filled up to the ceiling with choices and many variations of the same products, so much so that I became overwhelmed like never before, and I had to swiftly retreat from that place of extravagant choices, exhausted and empty handed, and go back to have a lie down, defeated.

This story is just an analogy to say that the amount of knowledge produced by both academia and business, regarding organisation and how they work, is vast and daunting, whilst paradoxically but understandably, it causes cynicism in those who may take a step back and say that regardless of that knowledge, most of the time we are left with results that are doubtful and certainly below the expectations and the costs that various change programs and related interventions have returned.

The world of business and particularly that of large corporations presents us with a vast and complex system in which the scale of issues can be equally challenging. At the same time, businesses have themselves made tremendous contributions to the knowledge of how they work, which is at least as important as that made by academics. This is because they have vast resources, not only financial but also human. The calibre of individuals who work in these organisations aggregates high standards of formal education, often across many specialist fields, and tremendous experiential knowledge exercised in extremely challenging, complex and innovative environments.

The result is the creation of high intellectual capital, intellectual property and many registered new patents, alongside methodologies and business practices, and a tremendous body of knowledge that is available to any member of the organisation, supported by competent mentors and role models and often structured learning through their own corporate academies. Together with established academia, this combination has produced and continues to produce a massive and valuable body of information.

And yet the question that is increasingly urgent, almost as a result of such vastness of resources is how to get back to basics. How do we make appropriate choices and use these specific approaches – out of all that is available – as needed and with a high chance the approach will work in the individual case of a specific organisation of a moderate size, with moderate resources, both human and financial?

And whilst we accept that the complexities of the outside world are more or less similar for all organisations, in all businesses and all enterprises, it is also true to say that there is a difference in complexity between an organisation employing 200,000 people across 25 countries or employing 250 people in one location. This is why some advantages of the difference in scale have to go in favour of the smaller organisations, in as far as the overall choice of approach is concerned. It is much easier to experience or envision a small – even if sophisticated – village rather than a metropolis.

In addition, smaller enterprises have a great opportunity to use the value of scientific and corporate expertise and knowledge, in an adapted and fit for purpose form, without the needs to make the same mistakes or invest the same resources to get the knowhow but simply assess their needs and adapt the best practice to their specific business model and purpose.

Guided by such considerations, I defined a model for the enterprises of the future. The structure of the model offers key references which define such an enterprise but can be interpreted and use flexibly in each case, depending on the business activity and the time in the life and history of the enterprise.

The model also allows for review and re-deployment to include agile new ways of re-designing the enterprise to flexibly respond to internal and external acting forces.

The outline of the model has been informed by science and theory that helped structure and formalise experiential findings. This approach is recognised by the scientist-practitioner framework and competencies, which align the outcomes of practice based modelling, in which practice informs science, as a complementary method to academic research in which models precede verification in practice.

Both practice and research approaches are based on science and generate knowledge that has for a long time been produced as a result of the same pursuit of professionalism and rigour that motivate different but complementary and equally valuable perspectives.

The architecture of the SOCIETALByDesign™ Model

For some decades now, I have been reflecting on the advancements in organisation development (O/D), the successes and failures of interventions aimed at influencing or correcting aspects of organisational life and the multitude of factors that are at work concurrently, some visible and some not. I have also watched how enterprises have changed and the impact of technology on leadership, management, work, skills and individuals.

The sense of awe at the dynamic complexities involved notwithstanding, I was looking for themes and patterns and something that was certain and remained stable in a sea of change. Surely, I thought there have to be things that we know and can do now, significant and impactful enough to steadily chip away at the edges of this compact jungle of entanglements and the vastness of relativities and interdependencies, where we do not seem to find that trail of crumbs that could lead us somewhere.

I could not help thinking that in fact, the answer has been in front of us all along, and we have always paid lip service to this factor but have not quite followed it through to business practice.

The importance of people is blatantly obvious, yet in so many cases, we have no focussed and consistent consideration for people even when rhetoric is impeccably scripted and articulated around the mantra "people are our most valuable asset" because we are busy with processes, procedures, technology and tangible operational bottom-line preoccupations.

In addition, I also noticed that the most basic principles that make people happy or unhappy, which common sense can teach us a lot about, and we need no research to back that up – although this is also available – gravitate around basic rules of human interaction and exchanges between people.

Finally, the turn of the 21st century has presented us with one of the most serious financial crises in decades. This was just the last irrefutable evidence that our society and economy were drifting away into uncharted and perilous waters to a new incarnation of the market economy, clearly set on a self-destruct path of ecological abuse and social inequity, that could not last long and took us to a point of no return. Opposing this were growing popular forces, scientists and other representatives of society and business increasingly taking positions in an attempt to stop this self-destructive drift. Here again the fundamental principles defended simple humanistic ideas of respecting the environment and handling responsibly our legacy to future generations.

All ideas converged towards a need to re-evaluate our hierarchies of importance and worth around the imperative of placing people at the centre of everything. This was my own conclusion in 2001 when I left the corporate world to dedicate my work to supporting and developing people in business because I had no doubt, based on my own extensive business experience, that this was the case.

The outcomes of such reflections have converged to give rise to the SOCIETALByDesign™ Model for successful adaptive enterprises of the digital age.

The thinking around the SOCIETALByDesign™ Model has been informed by:

- Several decades of international experience in business delivery and development of people in business
- A reflective supervised professional practice in business and management consulting
- Sustained and extensive continued professional development spanning a wide range of knowledge sources
- Polymath expertise across multiple disciplines and business functions
- Careful consideration of the challenges (ecological, political, social, economic) that the post-2009 decade has brought into the collective consciousness of business and social communities
- Appreciation of the ethical dilemmas and need to "rethink business as usual" in light of its negative social and ecological impacts that undermine sustainability and the future of next generations

Past experience and awareness of present challenges and opportunities have come together to inform the way we may envision the

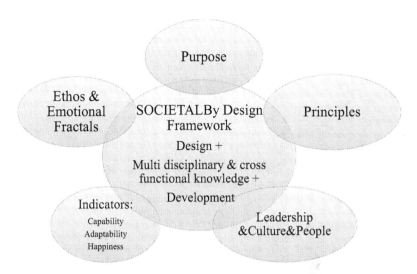

Figure 3.1 SOCIETALByDesign™ Model

future, to design and develop businesses that are fit for a newly defined purpose that respect humanistic values and respects the place and contributions that individuals and groups make in the seamlessly connected worlds of business and society.

What is good for business must not – going forward – harm individuals, society and nature. Instead it must enable, enhance and sustain the extraordinary value that human civilisation can achieve for the continued benefit to all.

What's in a name?

The word *SOCIETAL* is positioned in this model, as an acronym made of the initials of words (S – safe, O – open, C – collaboration, I – innovation, E – ethics, T – technology, A – accountability, L – legacy) that represent fundamental and necessary concepts which support the culture, philosophy and spirit of this model for organisation design and development, fit for adaptation in the digital age.

SOCIETAL culture responds the concerns and the pressures for change in the way businesses operate in the new millennium of integrated digital technologies because of their tremendous impact and the unintended and negative consequences that the business model exercised since the Third Industrial Revolution of 1969. This has evolved to create a type of market economy ruthlessly focussed on profit, which proved its lack of viability through the accumulation of pollution and depletion of natural resources alongside excessive risk-taking, polarisation of wealth and financial speculations which led to the financial crash of 2009.

This accumulation of multiple negative outcomes represent the current external pressures that demand of enterprises to change the way they operate, also as a result of the wider changes in the society represented by the millennial and the generations after them, who are now demanding systemic change.

The SOCIETALByDesign™ Model reflects these very concerns and positions a solution for a different way of operating in the market economy, led by the definition of purpose which embraces the inter-est of the enterprise top coincide with the best interest of the wider society and the planet.

The use of "ByDesign" in the name designates the fact that the ele-ments of the model have been carefully chosen for fitness of purpose, specifically, not by chance but by intention.

Framework

The SOCIETALByDesign™ Framework is made up of three elements (design, development, and the mixed body of knowledge coming from scientific disciplines and business functions, all introduced in the previous chapter): where the two strands of organisation design and O/D, each presents four complementary and symmetrical stages. In between them, there are the connections brought in by any num-ber of scientific disciplines and the typical business functions, which ensure the contents of knowledge that hold together the intercon-nected and complex vertical and horizontal dimensions which form an integrated, functional, adaptive structure that supports the life and evolution of an enterprise.

Far from being static, the two strands of design and development thinking and implementation are in fact helical and evolve together by connecting feedback loops, in a dynamic interaction that sees cycles of design, development, redesign and re-development in successive waves, with nodes of relative stability in between, that enable recovery and equilibrium, before the next iteration of change, through new design and development. These iterations are enabled and informed by an evolving body of knowledge coming from progress in science and business practice, which in turn also include changes that reflect the evolving social and cultural norms and the time and place of the prevailing human civilisation.

Table 3.1 SOCIETALByDesign™ Framework. O/D = organisation development

DESIGN / RE-DESIGN ART > Science ongoing	KNOWLEDGE Multi-disciplinary Cross-functional Art + Science + Technology evolving	DEVELOPMENT SCIENCE > Art ongoing
I. SPARK	*dialectics complexity supply chain* *project management sociology agile*	TRIGGER I.
II. IMMERSION	*quality gamification ethics*	ENQUIRY II.
III. ENVISIONING	*neuroscience employee engagement* *customer experience O/D marketing*	CONFIGURING III.
IV. REALISING	*design thinking philosophy culture*	DEPLOYMENT IV.

Note: O/D = organisation development

The design and development strands both contain science and art but in different degrees: in design, art prevails over science, whereas in development, science prevails over art. In the same way, the scientific disciplines and the business functions contain a combination or science and art. But in the scientific disciplines, science prevails over art, whereas in the business functions, art prevails over science.

The combined use of science and art in this model is necessary because all activity that involves people systems is a combination of precision and intuition, of fact and emotions, of the rational and subconscious, of the predictable and random, of the controllable and unintended.

The design strand of the framework contains the following four stages that combine science and art, precision and intuition which both define human cognition and action:

1   Spark: becoming alert and reacting to any event, opportunity, challenge or trigger that ignites the curiosity the engagement to all and any opportunities to review a situation that needs change and transformation, with an open mind, positive attitude and no judgements. Spark also includes curiosity, exploring with intuition, joy, positive emotions, openness, playfulness and lack of judgement. Spark is open minded, reflective and emotive.

2   Immersion: using the energy of the spark to explore with openness and curiosity the world of thoughts, emotions, needs, desires and actual experience of the potential beneficiaries or users,

exercising intuition, empathy, sympathy and playfulness "walking in their shoes" to best understand how to help the situation or develop the opportunity, going forward. Immersion is empathic, experiential and pragmatic.

3   Envisioning: considering a range of possibilities and alternatives that fit the purpose clarified during immersion, imagining answers to the question how can the best solution meet the needs or opportunities that have been identified and mapped through immersion, until the best of the potential solutions emerges and is mapped out to deliver most help, value and joy. Envisioning is cognitive, solution focussed and innovative.

4   Realising: translating the best solution into actions and applying it in the real situation. Realising is pragmatic, reasonable and joyous.

The development strand of the framework contains the following four stages:

1   Trigger: reacting to events or the field around the trigger event or the identified need for improvement and change. Identifying issues and causes. Holistic examination and data gathering from the entire organisation, to inform on mission, goals, policies, structures and technologies; climate and culture; environmental factors; desired outcomes and readiness to take action. Checking horizontal and vertical alignments and integration. Trigger is analytical, factual and immersive (in the organisation-specific environment).

2   Enquiry: exploring strategies and tactics for change and evaluating the feasibility of activities that are proposed for corrective actions. Designing a solution. Enquiry is empathetic, innovative and planned.

3   Configuring: the plan of action is being assigned to owners, change agents and sponsors, with detailed steps that are implemented whilst support and commitment from all is maintained. Progress is monitored. Configuring is structured, sympathetic and practical.

4   Deployment: implementing plans and assessing the planned change efforts by tracking the organisation's progress in implementing the change and by documenting its impact on the organisation. Deployment is evaluative, sympathetic and developmental.

In this framework, the design strand is considered to have a stronger artistic component (because it literally elicits imagination, play and creativity, as well as using creative artefacts to express ideas, drawing a lot from emotions and empathy, which nonetheless must eventually translate in factual and pragmatic outcomes), whereas the development strand is considered to have a more scientific component (because of the amount of science, research, tools and methodologies that are available but have to be used in a creative and adaptive way to a specific situation and make people believe in it and emotionally embrace it). In fact, both of them combine art and science but in different degrees.

In both design and development, the original stages of ideation and facts finding as well as the prototyping and solution development stages are informed by the prevalent science, arts, technology and cultural and social norms that reflect that stage of civilisation and therefore become representative for a particular point in time. This mixed body of knowledge creates a multidimensional mesh of connections between the two intertwined helical strands of enterprise design and development.

Whilst the framework can be clearly described with its various components presented in some order, this is just a simplified way of representing something complex by providing fixed points and notions of reference to make the understanding of the complexity of the business entity and its processes easier. In reality, the succession of stages in the two strands of design and development do not necessarily occur in a rigid succession, but the activity and the thinking involved can go back and forth between various stages.

In the same way, the contents of science and business practice, connecting design and development (the horizontal connections), may at times more precisely fit a particular stage of one or the other or both strands but may also reappear with various degrees of importance across all the segments of both (vertical) strands. In fact, whilst the framework may look like a ladder, in reality, it structures itself with a degree of entanglement. Both horizontal (body of knowledge) and vertical (design and development) integration, in between the main strands of design and development, are themselves interrelated.

This entanglement is due to the fact that the individuals, groups and enterprises are dynamic, changing, adaptive, evolving structures, as are the science and practice in between. These building blocks are constantly revisited in continuous transformative iterations that take the organisation from one state of being to another. Between these dynamic and repeated iterations, there are moments of equilibrium when the organisation finds its balance and operates at an optimum state for some time until internal or external forces cause it to revisit its structure and the way it works.

The overarching principle around the framework is that it represents a "map" for vertical and horizontal integration of complex processes within a complex system in which mechanisms such as feedback, connectivity, interdependence, co-evolution and creation of new order are at work. The result is an enterprise that maintains its integrity as an entity but is constantly changed over time, just like a river may exist over millennia whilst constantly changing its course, the outline of its banks and the depth or the quality of its water at the same time.

People bring businesses to life: enabling human energy to flow and flourish

Since the Third Industrial Revolution (1969 – information technology and electronics revolution) and particularly the decade of the 1980s, the external environment has become turbulent and disrupted with change and technology-led transformations that have accelerated at an unprecedented pace. The economy today is globalised, and businesses find themselves in the eye of an endless web of connectivity, subject to forces of entropy from outside and within. Interdependence and interconnectivity have given rise to tremendous complexity and a new world defined by volatility, uncertainty, complexity and ambiguity. In this world, it is no longer possible to establish where causality starts or ends.

The world of business and the global economy have moved to a new paradigm where the customers are at the centre of attention and power, whilst businesses are rethinking and re-designing themselves in ways to best serve the consumers. The quality and the range of products and services have now changed to connect them to digital capabilities that increase accessibility and value. Technology now makes assets more durable and resilient, whilst data analytics has changed the way they are used and maintained.

This is a world where customer experience, product and service performance, data analytics and disrupted business models all demand the rethinking of the way we collaborate and innovate to meet challenges brought about by change. Change has also brought opportunities that have seen the birth of new services, expectations, skill sets and jobs in what is a complete transformation of the entrepreneurial landscape.

As a result, employee engagement and employee experience, along technological platforms that enable recruitment and development of talent and changes in culture, expectations and organisational forms have seen an inevitable need for review.

The case for an ethical business purpose

To understand how abstraction meets reality in the field and how the link between purpose and achievement of established enterprise objectives match or not, it is useful to refer to recent history and look at the example of the financial crises of 2009. This crisis seriously eroded the confidence in business, institutions, governments and governance, to a point from where it has still not recovered one decade later. A very interesting argument was being put forward by the parties involved in the UK Select Committee's enquiry at the time, for example, which called the parties involved in the crash to account. These parties were bank CEOs, auditors, rating agencies, the financial services authority (FSA) and the big accounting firms. These parties put forward the following circular blame argument:

- The accountants said that they only took snapshots of figures at points in time and could not on such bases predict future outcomes, so they blame the auditors for not spotting the cracks.
- The auditors argued that they could only access audit reports information as it was presented to them by management; therefore, the banks were to blame for withholding critical information.
- The banks replied by blaming the FSA for not giving them a better guidance on what documents to present to auditors.
- The FSA replied by blaming the government for not giving them enough power and clearer guidance, and therefore they themselves had relied on the auditors and rating agencies to flag risks.
- The rating agencies blamed the auditors and the accountants for presenting to them figures which indicated that organisations were "healthy", and this led them into giving triple ratings to banks that were in fact failing, so the blame now return to banks for publishing figures which were not properly audited at the time of publication.
- The banks – back in the blame loop – looked at the CEO for answers and explanations.
- The CEOs replied by not accepting the burden of responsibility and instead squarely blamed . . .
- The business model!

And so the blame game finally rested with the business model, and the enquiry halted in its tracks somewhat abruptly, in the face of this final argument pointing the finger at some abstract thing instead of someone.

And whilst – if it were not such a serious matter – one may consider this a funny, if somewhat dark, example of resolution at the end of a serious enquiry – this is no laughing matter, and the devastating impact that irresponsible business practice has had on millions of people is still with us a decade later.

The resting point of the enquiry is an important one, too, because it opens another set of even more interesting questions:

- Is a business model an act of nature like a volcanic eruption or a tsunami?
- Or is it an act of creative human ingenuity in the pursuit of business instrumentation? And if so, what labyrinth of rabbit holes may this lead to?

And if so, one may take the view that the culprit business model in question is in fact directly linked to the mission and objectives of a business. And when the mission is to make as much profit as possible regardless of impacts, this indeed explains how the indicted business model became the blunt instrument for implementing a philosophy utterly lacking ethics by design. With the clear intention that ethical consideration for individuals, society or environment are not on the agenda of the company, it set for itself a narrow focus and unique objective of profit by all means.

This narrow business focus is why, whilst some acknowledgement was given to shared responsibility for the financial disaster, actual regret, apologies and recognition of their involvement and responsibility were not as clear and as forthcoming as we would have expected even from a common person in the street, let alone from leaders of multibillion financial operations.

Furthermore, today there are many signs that the risks taken then in the pursuit of profit are again building up in spite of some measures put in place after 2009, whilst CEOs of financial and other organisation genuinely think that they fully deserve remunerations and bonuses of hundreds of millions even when holding the CEO position for short periods of time and leading companies that are clearly failing, according to indicators recognised even by them. We are far from having resolved this problem.

Perhaps defining a "business model" that aligns to a purpose that is positioned in the first instance where it should be – in the service of people and with ethics in the design – will save us all the embarrassment of arguments that really defy common sense and our natural inclination for fairness.

Let us align the rest of the business model's interdependent and co-evolving factors such as mission, vision, strategy and objectives to a purpose that does not insult the collective sense of decency and social equity, principles that the bright side of our human nature and civilisation has also refined and deployed in so many progressive ways for the benefit of a multitude of environments and people.

The purpose of SOCIETALByDesign™ Enterprises: being part of the solution and not creating or adding to exiting problems

SOCIETALByDesign™ Enterprises exist to enable people to utilise skill, competencies, capabilities and aspirational drivers in an environment where their engagement, and their work contributes to sufficient revenue generation that can fulfilling their material, spiritual and creative needs, as well as contributing to providing answers or resolving problems that concern the wider society. In this way, individual lives as well as the continued existence of the human civilisation, in its created and natural environments, are sustained by eliminating threats and potential harms to people and environments, enabling human existence and civilisation to continue and flourish.

Sufficient revenue can be flexibly defined as deicide by the business to be either enough to cover costs or to provide additional money that can be reinvested in the business or placed elsewhere, where it may resolve needs of the society. Revenue is realised by commercial activities that sell products and services of any kind, in line with the organisations purpose. Revenue-generating methods themselves do not harm society (e.g. products and services sold are not detrimental to customers and their well-being or the environment).

By exercising a first duty to their own staff, such enterprises take care of thousands of people and their dependents, a section of the wider society that is provided income, support for families and dignified and purposeful lives for many who otherwise may become problems for society because of unemployment, low income and poor quality of life. Generating enough revenue to cover operating costs that include salaries and maintenance of good working conditions and terms of employment (which can be set as business goals), the SOCIETALByDesign™ Enterprise fulfils its purpose and "walks the talk" within its own boundaries.

If revenue is set to exceed the operating costs (which can also be set as a business objective) needed to ensure a good quality of employment for employee and contributors, this can be directed outside the organisation to the wider society in many forms that in turn must not do harm and directly contribute to resolution of already exiting problems.

By not exacerbating existing concerns and actively contributing to safeguarding the well-being and equilibrium of the wider social and ecological systems, businesses will not only serve the people who work in those but will also collectively create an economic network in which what is good for society is good for business and what the business delivers to customers is good for society.

The focus of the SOCIETALByDesign™ Enterprise shifts from making profit and encouraging consumerism to measuring business success via the happiness and well-being of its employees alongside reduction of problems that society is facing. The profit-at-all-costs alternative often includes high utilisation of natural resources as well as stimulating a culture of "fast acquisition of disposable items", encourages spending, and more often than not, high individual debts and also embeds habits and sometimes addictions undermining public health and well-being. A non-SOCIETALByDesign™ enterprise treats these as externalities to their bottom line or possibly even benefits.

The objective of SOCIETALByDesign™ Enterprises is one in which the focus is not on profit at any cost to others but on business success achieved by respectfully realising the full potential of every person in work and the ethical management of the overall human talent, including the impact of externalities.

SOCIETALByDesign™ Enterprise have to be "by design" best places to work and will attract a certain type of people: people who care about ethics and self-realisation; who want to experience fair and structured support to focus and get on with being happy at work (duvet flappers who can't wait to get up in the morning) and deliver their best contributions; who do not want to waste creative vitality or be ground down by concerns about bonuses, working overtime to be seen to be keen, having to give the pound of flesh for promotions and financial incentives, and all the other well researched factors of disengagement and stress that plague employees in conventional profit-driven organisations.

Instead the SOCIETALPeople appreciate sufficient and fair pay, recognition, collaborations, training and career progression opportunities, being allowed a degree of self-determination and autonomy and being encouraged to meaningfully develop and grow, to enjoy work in the company of others.

SOCIETALByDesign™ dynamic principles

The Fourth Industrial Revolution has impacted business by focussing priorities on customer expectation, innovation, collaboration and employee engagement, product and service development and enhancement and the rethinking of organisational structure, function and development. And this is just an overview of the complex external forces that have been pressing businesses to reinvent themselves.

But inside the organisation, things do not remain static because the organisation in fact holds any number of people who are themselves complex evolving and changing systems driven by their individual purpose and drive for meaning, values and beliefs, which change over time because of individual experience, age and changes of personal circumstances. As a result, individuals do not remain the same during the tenure of their employment with an organisation, particularly if they stay with an organisation for years.

The changes that are both unplanned and planned consciously and often subconsciously may cause an individual to become more or less engaged with the organisation. Combined with the trust and the psychological contract between individuals and organisations, broken, as it has been in the past fifteen years or so, it is not surprising that loyalty and employee engagement have been subjects of concern for some time.

So how can we contemplate such complexity with a degree of structure, and what existing models can we use? Today more than ever before, the dialectic thinking and the principles of complex evolving systems theory have come into their own, helping us make sense of change, complexity and evolution by providing guiding models and philosophical and scientific frameworks and principles to this end. Dialectics and complexity thinking have been introduced as excellent and pertinent references fit for our world, and it is useful to translate such knowledge to define a set of dynamic principles applicable in the SOCIETALByDesign™ Model of an adaptive agile enterprise.

In addition, the dynamic principles of this model are informed by multidisciplinary and cross-functional bodies of knowledge available today to business practitioners. They also reflect the multifold influences of human nature and civilisation that manifest within organisational life, just as in the wider society which combines the following items:

- *Biological dimension*: the foundation essential to keep us alive individually and ensure the continuity of humans as the life form on our planet
- *Psychological dimension:* an emergent result from the evolution of the nervous system and the brain, which enables the manifestation of our individual psyche, as an advanced evolved interface for relating with each other and the outside world

- *Social dimension:* this represents our specific human capability of abstract thinking and communicating through language with our fellow human beings, in group and collective which together generate culture and cultural artefacts and which uniquely enables us collectively to benefit from the advantage of social cultural accumulation
- *Philosophical, ethical and meaning making dimension:* which elevates us above other known complex life forms because of our need and capability to mentally travel through time and space and critically analyse, ask and answer questions about our place in the universe and the past, present and future of the universe itself.

In real life and business, however, all these aspects are by no means neatly differentiated and bounded but are intertwined and unfold as a coherent emergence and an outcome greater and more complex than the sum of parts. The order of precedence is not hierarchical because all aspects are equally important and can become critical factors for success or failure at different points in time, depending on many factors including context. However, some factors are more predicable than others, and biological factors need specific attention because of their mainly unconscious nature and swift impact on individual and collective cognition and behaviour.

Equally, the dynamic principles of the SOCIETALByDesign™ Model that follow reflect the complex facets of an enterprise identity, created by its collective human element. They, too, cross over rigid categorisation for the very reason that reality as such is not always ordered in the way we can order information through our critical thinking. The core dynamic principles interact and manifest at all times and are supported by other dynamic micro and macro factors which play important roles but have not been singled out because they may be known and unknown, and their number can potentially be infinite, depending on the level of granularity that we wish to employ.

The core working dynamic principles identified for the SOCIETAL-ByDesign™ Model follow, with brief explanations of what they mean in the context of this specific model and the overarching message of the book. All the principles directly connect to a multidisciplinary and cross-functional body of knowledge that has already been introduced.

These principles range from philosophy and ethics; to psychology and social sciences, neuroscience and decision making; to business, project and quality management; to definitions of purpose, vision and mission; to exercise of leadership and embodied culture.

The new societal organisation design and re-design and development must also respond to the urgent call to action coming from the wider society, to review global economic paradigms, to become part of the solution to ecological and sustainability threats and safeguard our legacy to future generations instead of blindly and ruthlessly pursuing profits in the short term and at the cost of relentless depletion of irreplaceable resources and irreversible pollution.

First principle: complexity and dialectic evolution

SOCIETALByDesign™ Enterprises are complex systems dynamically driven by combined dialectic and complexity principles and vehicles of adaptive and evolutionary transformations.

Organisations, no matter how large or small, are complex systems because in today's globalised economy, every enterprise is part of the wider economy and society – local or global – and therefore interdependent on other participants in its critical supply and value path These organisations are also local or global, and their own complexity – in turn – may vary and change. Therefore, organisations are subject to complex evolving systems dynamic principles as well as all other principles operating in reality itself.

Dialectic thinking posits that the world is constantly transforming and moving, subject to dynamic change, with only relative static stages and full of complex processes of transformation coming into being and passing away, moving from lower to higher states by quantitative accumulations. This process results in new qualitative stages, just like a knotted line in which the station of a knot enables accumulation of quantity before moving onto the next level of quality.

Dialectic thinking also offers the concept of triads, or a third option (thesis, antithesis and synthesis), as the dynamic principle of progression, in which one state is challenged by another and the result is yet another state that emerges as a result of the mixing of the two. In the process, some of the old being developed, some cast out and some totally new attributes brought forward. In this way, legacy as well as the present and the future are all linked in hidden connections at any point in time, even if not visible.

In light of reality, the way we now look for the third option and aim to introduce it in computing, alongside the insufficient binary dichotomy of yes/no, 0/1, certainty/uncertainty, the introduction of the third "I don't know" or "both" option, becomes imperative as a direct reflection of our uncertain reality.

In plain language, it means that we need to stop looking for certainty and linear causality, accept uncertainty and complexity and start developing new ways to remain effective and focussed on what we know and can see right now, to build resilience and expect the

unexpected with confidence in our ingenuity instead of anxiously cry-
ing wolf.

*Second principle: feedback loops, self-regulation
and helical iterations*

SOCIETALByDesign™ Enterprises are systems that can exercise varying degrees of self-direction and self-rebalancing if and when enabled by feedback loops and agile helical iterations set in motion by a
purpose-driven leadership and culture by using the significant body of
knowledge provides by a multidisciplinary cross-functional approach,
to a solution focussed problem solving.

Depending on the identity of each organisation and its wider systems, there are activities and structures that can be fully controlled,
others in which control diminishes to be replaced by a possibility
to influence and finally others in which there is no control at all.
All degrees of control manifest concurrently and can be planned
or unplanned. Providing reflective processes and feedback loops
will enable self-corrections in real time and open the possibility for
dynamic controls through agile helical iterations.

Enterprises can exercise a lot of control by utilising the knowledge
from management, quality and project management methodologies.
These not only offer fundamental practical approaches but have also
moved with the times to reflect the consideration of agility and complex thinking in enterprise dynamics. The body of tools, methods
and models provided by such sciences and practice is significant and
coherently works together.

All practitioners need to do is to refer to the vast body of knowledge
that exists and use specialists and polymaths and work across disciplines and teams, to choose and create a best of breed and fit for purpose methodology that reflects the specific needs identity and stage in
the life-cycle of the enterprise. They offer a very significant possibility
of control through processes procedure, policies, tools and technologies that could be used in the work environment to provide stability.

There isn't a lot of complexity or difficulty in accepting that good
and healthy workplaces, with adequate tools and processes that enable
people to do their work without hindrance is totally under the control of enterprise leaders and senior managers. And this already sets
a solid platform for better response to the environment than activity that we know and also for unforeseen circumstances. In addition,
there is a significant body of knowledge that comes from psychology,
behavioural psychology and social sciences that offer information

about options to influence human emotions, motivation, indivisible drivers and mood.

This directly links to the way the enterprise has set up its policies, its feedback loops and its inclusion and recognition of collective and individual contributions to the quality of work and to the creation of innovative solutions to problems for all. People who actually do the work always know how things are and what can be improved and if they are only given the chance and the trust to have a voice and contribute they could solve many problems.

This again consolidates the capability of the enterprise to work with known and unknown circumstances. Controlling the mood of the organisation results in a power of influence, which in turn can yield back tangible positive outcomes that contribute to the strengths of the enterprise through the collective positive emotional and aspirational ethos that can be influenced and eventually does contribute to an increased level of control of organisational dynamics.

With all such fundamentals in place, the resilience of the organisation is greatly increased to face flexibly and adaptively the need for controlled change and the response to unforeseen unpredictable circumstances. After decades of research and centuries of practice, we have today vast amounts of knowledge which is not used as well has it could be. And this may be one clear approach to uncertainty rather than emphasising the volatility and lack of predictability that we tend to put forward as factors over which we do not have control and deport ourselves in an unnecessary state of this dis-empowerment.

Third principle: business success is about solutions
and serving the good of society

SOCIETALByDesign™ Enterprises designed and developed around the ethical value that "what makes society thrive is good for business" are evolved businesses that that have become "solutions" to the problems unleashed by the destructive pursuit of profit, which threaten the continuity of human civilisation.

Ethics is about morality, justice and what course of action to take in particular situations. It is an extensive branch of philosophy and covers:

Meta ethics: as a theoretical frame of meaning and moral proposition and how their true value can be determined
Normative ethics: looking at practical ways to determine a moral course of actions

Applied ethics: regarding what an individual is allowed or compelled to do in a specific situation and domain of action

In organisations, the ethical aspect of business acquires an added dimension beyond the immediate human aspect because of its economic, political and ecological impact. An enterprise is a complex set of activities and arrangements, which is effectively influenced by activity type and the collective purpose towards which all the individuals who are part of the enterprise converge. Purpose can be defined to be just inwards looking or outwards looking to society and the planet.

SOCIETALByDesign™ Enterprises take responsibility for the wider context because of their impact on suppliers, clients, the market, governance systems and so on because the product and services that they provide reach further out into a much wider and often global human community. Therefore, it becomes clear that introducing ethical awareness everywhere in the organisation and particularly at every step of processes that lead to outcomes which impact others in the right or wrong way is a necessity in as far as preventing the wrong course of action and negative impact on others as well as a real sense of participation to deciding on ethical outcomes.

SOCIETALByDesign™ Enterprise redefines sustainability and instead of its current triple bottom-line measure of financial, social and environmental risks – also known as 3Ps, profit, people, and planet – repositions it as revenue, people and planet. The social inequity that the pursuit of profit has caused is triggering our hardwired reaction to rebel against unfairness and injustice, and we instinctively react when we see infringements of what we perceive as basic mechanisms of maintaining fairness.

In a SOCIETALByDesign™ Enterprise, adherence to ethical principles is business as usual and ensures that the outputs to society, as well as their path of production and distribution, are based on ethical principles that employees understand and uphold. This, in my experience, is not normally the case; the conversation about ethics is rarely conducted at every step of business with the focus being rather on the pragmatism of business objectives and business profitability.

Ethics should not only be part of the boardroom conversations, even if it is the natural starting place, but should be embodied and encouraged by the leadership throughout the entire organisation. We have examples in the public domain in which leadership has broken its ethical obligations behaving in ways that frankly confused if not disabled the moral compass of employees in the organisation, providing destructive feedback loops and being examples of what not to do and how not to behave rather than positive role models. Ultimately, unethical behaviour is self-destructive to an organisation, whether it starts from its employees, leadership or the world at large.

In the SOCIETALByDesign™ Enterprise, one of the key roles of leaders is to develop purpose, values and beliefs, mission and vision that should rest on ethical principles and should be embraced by the entire organisation. With an ethically guided leadership in place, it is necessary that ethics are visible and seen to be embodied from the top down to enable and foster an uncompromising culture of trust and ethical business conduct.

Fourth principle: quality thinking is a strategic tool

The quality philosophy of the SOCIETALByDesign™ vertically integrates its purpose, strategy and implementation and seamlessly connects the enterprise, its people and its outputs with the people and the needs of the wider society.

The definition of quality is not linear and straightforward because quality is a subjective construct, an expectation that individuals or groups of individuals build and wish to attain, partly dependent on individual choices, party linked to group memes and in modern times, very much linked to advertising and social media.

Marketing born in the 50s and 60s was very much based – as it is still today – on psychological factors and the ability of advertising to induce and create dreams and wants by manipulating the unconscious to influence buying behaviours for commercial gains and profit.

Based on implicit associations, quality reflects values, beliefs, anxieties, wants, desires and fantasies of people and as such is a "fata morgana", a "chimera" or a construct of the mind.

The connection between the mind and the tangible is made through fitness for purpose positioning quality as being aligned with an outcome or a specification and has initially been used by quality theorists and practitioners in relation to manufacturing and the expectation that a product or service fulfils its purpose as defined by the needs and desires of the beneficiaries or the goals of the providers or other agencies that set standards and norms.

What is striking in all these consideration is the human factor, subjective and volatile that links those who provide and those who receive. And this is critical for a SOCIETALByDesign™ Enterprise, in which the concept of quality can be designed and positioned strategically in both internal and external terms for the needs of employees and those of the wider society.

In the SOCIETALByDesign™ Enterprise, quality must specifically align to its purpose and focus on the way the enterprise treats its own talent, the employee experience and the design and development of the enterprise to serve and support its people in the first instance. The quality philosophy of the SOCIETALByDesign™ Enterprise has to envision and embody values and belief, purpose and vision, culture and leadership that are generally people focussed and in which ideas are led by example and the proof and implementation start "at home".

Happy and engaged employees can only create products and services designed with the recipients in mind and their happiness. In this sense, quality is a horizontal and vertical internal integrator as well as a strategic instrument in the achievement of purpose.

Fifth principle: openness to internal and external
feedback and listening loops

The adaptive SOCIETALByDesign™ enterprise is an open listening systems, capturing external signals from suppliers, competitors, partners, clients and the wider society on potential disruption, opportunities and threats; internally listening to its people for opportunities to improve employees experience; and fine tuning the capability to pursue purpose and objectives without derailments.

It is only natural that whilst working in constantly changing, competing and evolving organisations, both staff and leaders become absorbed with the business at hand and concentrate on the good workings of the organisation to deliver their promise to their market. And because this internal process is complex and demanding, it is very easy to become self-absorbed, stay with an inward-looking lens and become somewhat impermeable or uninterested in all the buzz and the activity outside organisational boundaries.

However, it is absolutely necessary that every organisation, no matter how large or small, has intelligence scouts out in the wider field that return information from competitors, clients, suppliers, regulators, industry and professional bodies and society at large. And this is because the wider system is in itself a system that needs management and regulation and develops in controlled and uncontrolled circumstances. As a result, there are constant changes that occur, some of which can be incredibly important for the smaller world of the enterprise.

Changes in technology, skills availability, labour laws, regulation and global trends in the enterprise's specific markets are of particular interest because they can derail the current balance and potential success or can bring opportunities for a business that may be declining to provide clarity on future strategy to adapt and survive.

SOCIETALByDesign™ Enterprises should be connected to the wider world, listening and critically analysing information, to be used by leaders and the rest of the organisation to stimulate feedback. This will generate collective engagement and energy to use what is relevant in the best possible way to serve the organisation whether it wishes to expand or consolidate or maintain current stability. Sources of such information are in the public domain, professional associations and organisations, conferences, publications, government briefings, social media special-interest groups, think tanks and so on.

Looking internally, the most frequent complaint that people have in private and work environments is captured in one statement repeated so many times: "It would have been nice to be told . . ." or "It would have been nice to have been asked before you made a decision about my work . . ." And it is because this need of being consulted connects at a much deeper level with our values and beliefs and our need for positive emotions brought about by being respected, acknowledged, accepted as part of the group, empowered to have a voice and invited to participate even when we may not have something to say or we wouldn't voice our views even if invited.

In a SOCIETALByDesign™ Enterprise, the relationships that managers and leaders have with their staff has to be based on trust and respect and communicate throughout the organisation in all directions, including accepting opinions, ideas, suggestions, critiques and criticisms as part of a healthy internal communications network that should be able to constantly bring to the surface potential risks and opportunities, take the pulse of the organisational mood and provide early warnings for the leaders to deal with, as well as enthusiastic and positive energy that can be immediately directed to constructive use.

Sixth principle: integration of art, science and technology

Art, science and technology are all mandatory elements of the SOCIETALByDesign™ enterprise business processes and outcomes, necessary to balance emotion, reason and innovation, to respect and celebrate humanity and use the full and complex potential of people, within and outside the enterprise.

Innovation and creativity are key survival capabilities carried by human imagination and the world of emotions and thought that together provide outcomes of exceptional complexity and value that can satisfy the mind and move the soul. Science is steeped in imagination and the belief in possibilities but then moves on the path of reason and proof. Technology takes science and applies it in ways that can be utilised by many people to improve their lives and tame nature.

When reason and applied science run out of energy, art is called in to imagine and again push the boundaries of what is possible, to continue the evolutionary cycle that never stops. People's connection with the world runs though emotions and fantasy, and ignoring this tremendous positive force comes at the cost of making our life experience poorer. In fact, it is impossible because artistic expression has found its way in human society as early as cave dwellers some 40,000 years ago who were able for the first time to mark stone walls with imprints of hands and contours of animals.

Art is part of the human hard-wired identity, and societies and enterprises that do not celebrate and nurture it are poorer for it. Innovation, creativity and inventions are all related to art, and the power of the imagination is at its origin. All such activities are interconnected and co-emergent. Many of the scientific advancements have been catalysed by moments when thinkers have been inspired by surrounding stimuli of an aesthetic and artistic nature such as shapes seen in landscapes or the skies and the way those abstract stimuli have been interpreted by human imagination and creativity to then lead to a translation into hard science and technology.

Art connects to emotions, dreaming, imagining and meaning; science is about cognition and reason, understanding the underlying principles of nature and existence; whilst technology carries the benefits of both into the quality of life of many people and becomes part of the human civilisation and its artefacts. They represent a reflection of the multifold nature of humanity, biological, psychological, social and philosophical. SOCIETALByDesign™ Enterprises create an environment where these aspects manifest, aligned by the purpose of being in the service of people and society at large.

Use of skills and capabilities serves cognition and achievement, creativity and innovation are fuelled by positive emotions and applied in purposeful design. The collective capabilities of teams and networks envision and deliver goods and services by using the advancements of science and technology and as a result of bringing art, science and technology together, realising revenue and benefiting people all around.

Seventh principle: restrictions on diverse human talent
is the highest risk to enterprises

SOCIETALByDesign™ Enterprises are adaptive and can prevail over many types of adversity and shortages except for restrictions on people on which they are singularly dependent and which represent the single highest risk. This talent must be diverse and include specialists, generalists, polymaths and social sciences practitioners.

Organisation cannot be set up without an initial level of capability good enough to get the business off the ground without any significant or at least small and manageable short-term losses. Capability precedes development and performance in that it states the possibility of a business to operate. Capability is maintained or enhanced by development and maturity through time and continued learning and transformation.

This must include diversity of talent from specialist to polymaths and from hard science to social sciences practitioners, operating within a clear ethical framework that advises the deployment of expertise and creativity, to support ongoing innovation and to best enable human potential to flourish, with a defined purpose of a higher level and with the good of many in mind.

Capability remains a key indicator at all times, attesting that the enterprise has the resources it needs at the level of experience and ability it needs to run a good business and achieve its objectives as soon as it is set up. Future changes and adaptations can be achieved with similar resources by adding resources or by changing the mix of required resources in different ways. But capability remains the central indicator regarding the ability of a business to execute its objectives, whatever they may be and however they may change over time.

Not all organisational resources can develop, including people who may or may not embrace continued change and learning as positioned from the outside. In SOCIETALByDesign™ Enterprises, maintaining capability is an aspiration that should drive both the enterprise and individuals in work and should be nurtured by extrinsic and intrinsic motivators. Human resources (HR) must make training and development available, whilst individuals should take up such offers to gain personal enrichment but also contribute to the collective capability advantage of the enterprise.

This is why at any point in time, organisations need of assess current capability and plug any gaps by any methods or channels, including hiring capable resources by various flexible contribution arrangements, whilst waiting for the time it may take for internal resources to take up developmental opportunities or to skill up.

As a key indicator in SOCIETALByDesign™ Enterprises, organisational capability always inform the enterprise on its need to develop skills or to supplement them and so maintain a dynamic balance of what is immediately available and what not, so that the capability indicator is never below a set level.

Eighth principle: individuals and groups are equally influential

The destiny of a SOCIETALByDesign™ enterprise can be equally determined by individuals or by groups because in the complex enterprise dynamics, individuals are as important as groups and groups are as important as individuals.

We all know from history or experience that individuals have made a significant impact on groups and charted the course of the future. Such individuals are leaders and influencers that capture the mood and the spirit of a time, a place and a collective mood, and exercise impact on those around them because of many factors, which range from individual personality traits, to specific life experience, attribute of power or charisma.

It is a fact that as individuals, we are all unique, and whilst we share similar traits with other individuals, we are nonetheless talented and flawed in a particular way which makes us who we are and gives us our specific identity. This identity is made of our instinctive reactions and basic emotions, the values and beliefs which have developed on top of those basic neurological structures, our acquisition of skills, our professional and life experience, the way we communicate and behave and our capability to influence others. In addition, leaders also need to be able to connect and relate to the wider culture and the group they are leading and commence their transformational mission from where everyone else is to take them to where the implementation of a shared vision needs them to be.

We are all able to influence others and groups either in an active or a passive way. Even holding a position of neutrality and following others are also mechanisms of individually influencing groups and outcomes. This is why it is important to pay attention to individuals and be able to assess, evaluate, prevent or proactively utilise their capabilities and their roles in groups.

The power of groups is self-evident if only by the simple factor of critical mass. Throughout history, there are examples of when groups have changed the course of events, unseated the status quo and have led to bloody and violent convulsions of the social and political nature. Groups can undermine the best of plans and the best of ideas and are subject to deep, mainly unconscious, dynamic forces that from this single collective well can lead to amazing construction or utter destruction.

Groups exercise a powerful influence over individuals because they embody the culture of a group or organisation and act as custodians of boundaries to values, beliefs and behaviours held within it. They also impose a code of communication and conduct to everyone that finds themselves caught – willingly or not – within its boundaries.

Groups give rise to territoriality, rivalries, tribal allegiances and abuse of power under the leadership of individuals who know how to use this energy and who can appeal to the very powerful collective unconscious drivers of fear, anger or sadness and utilise it for good or for ill.

This is why in the SOCIETALByDesign™ Enterprises, individuals and groups, leaders and teams hold equal status and are all subjects of interest in enterprise design and development. Both culture and leadership start with bringing into the organisations the right and fit for purpose individual talent followed by development and integration of multidisciplinary and cross-functional effective and agile teams that create a culture which matches the ideals expressed and embodied by leadership.

Ninth principle: safeguarding physical and mental well-being

Physical and mental well-being and safety in the workplace are critical factors of a SOCIETALByDesign™ Enterprise success and have to be aligned to purpose, ethics, values and objectives.

Physical and mental well-being is served by general factors such as personal and emotional development and self-awareness; a stable personal, socio-economic and work environment; the ability to cope and overcome temporary setbacks without lasting negative consequences; a good diet and a healthy life style; enjoyment of time off and time to relax; the presence of purpose, meaning and fulfilment; and a sense of humour and connectedness to others. These are all positive contributing factors to one's good general and mental health. And this is something that by definition a SOCIETALByDesign™ organisation is committed to do in line with its purpose.

But actual mental illness is a responsibility of the wider society, and mental health in organisations is a subset of the bigger system. Government and charities are making good progress in their effort to diminish the stigma related to mental illness. And whilst organisations can pioneer good practice, it rests with the wider society and prevailing local and global culture to make the changes necessary on a much greater scale.

Organisations, just like society at large, have a mixed and diverse population within, which is bound to contain individuals with psychological and psychiatric issues. The assumption that organisations are "mental illness free" flies in the face of the reality, which suggests that the pathological landscape of society will also leave a footprint on the organisational landscape.

What may be specific to organisations is that they are smaller communities with greater individual visibility, and therefore, stigma, shame and lack of understanding may be more apparent because of the close working relationships between colleagues.

This is why having a process in place to facilitate the way people that need understanding and support can be identified and encouraged to be further referred to relevant specialists is mandatory whilst at the same time not crossing the boundaries between what enterprises are not qualified to do. The boundaries of professional ethics have to be in place for HR, coaches, trainers, facilitators, consultants and other professionals working in the enterprise space to know where their expertise ends.

Mental health has always been and remains a subject of concern for the wider society and the prevailing culture: a solution can be found by an alliance between many contributors each with their domain of expertise because we are dealing with a multidisciplinary and cross-functional challenge.

In antiquity, epileptic fits (which are in fact neurological disorders rather than mental disorders) were considered moments of divine intervention, and this condition made the people who had it special because they were in touch with the divine. Fast forward to the Middle Ages, and epilepsy became the playground of the devil. Equally, scientists and progressive thinkers could be burned to the stake for challenging the existing order.

In the 17th to 19th centuries, Europe relatives could declare a member of the family as unstable and have them sectioned for life in "lunatic asylums", a very neat way for those with power and interest to be rid of those who may have challenged their deeds. Any deviation from the prevailing norms set for society by individuals or groups in power were seen as undesirable and dealt with swiftly and mercilessly. Mental health was a political weapon, equally used today with political dissidents of modern time.

But today science is on our side, and we know so much more, yet in the 21st century, there are still regions on the globe where the old mentality is entrenched and people with mental illness are seen as possessed by evil forces. Mental health issues will not be resolved by organisations alone but by society.

However, enterprises can and must exercise a duty of care to protect, prevent, assist, not cause illness and not collude in any way with retrograde views and practices. Instead enterprises must support education, research and change of culture in business and society at large, starting with their own people. And this is something that every business can do, without a doubt.

Tenth principle: eliminate or mitigate enterprise toxicity

SOCIETALByDesign™ Enterprises acknowledge that actual human nature is ambivalent, and its dark side manifests in thinking biases, maladaptive personalities and default biological reactions that must be constantly monitored and mitigated to prevent or reduce organisational toxicity.

Our lofty aspirations, our curiosity, our desire for exploration and our capability for higher purpose and meaning making have kept our gaze looking into the future from the penthouse of the soaring edifice of our civilisation, whilst down in the basement, the forces of nature have continued to do their work, which also contributes to our surviving and thriving, in very complex settings but equally undermine the flight of our best intentions and aspirations when we least expect.

Amongst these challenges, there are aspects related to personality development – known as the dark triad – and unconscious thinking biases, which impact our cognition.

The dark triad refers to the specific personality traits of machiavellianism, narcissism and psychopathy or sociopathy.

Machiavellianism in psychology (coined by 1970s social psychologists Richard Christie and Florence L. Geis) refers to a personality trait which sees a person so focussed on their own interests they will manipulate, deceive and exploit others to achieve their goals.

Narcissistic personality disorder (NPD) is a personality disorder with a long-term pattern of behaviour with exaggerated feelings of self-importance, excessive need for admiration and preoccupation with appearance, lack of empathy and fixation on how to achieve success and power by taking advantage of the people around to this end.

Psychopathy also synonymous with sociopathy is a personality disorder characterised by persistent antisocial behaviour. Significant traits include boldness (toleration of unfamiliarity, danger and stress; high self-confidence; and social assertiveness), dis-inhibition (poor impulse control, lacking emotions, demand for immediate gratification and poor behavioural restraints) and meanness (lacking empathy and close attachments, use of cruelty to gain empowerment, exploitative tendencies, defiance of authority, and destructive excitement seeking)

Unconscious thinking biases are mechanisms that impede our cognitive functions or ability to think rationally without being derailed and driven to incorrect conclusions or decisions. The list of such biases is long and continually growing, but some of the known examples are in-group bias, herd instinct, halo effect, egocentric bias, projection bias and self-serving bias, to name just a few.

Human personality and modalities of adaptation to society and life are diverse, and even if small, the number of people that can negatively impact the life of organisations is likely to be there. Business settings are often seen as fields full of opportunity, where attributes such as focus, pragmatism, competitiveness and single-minded pursuit of objectives are encouraged and celebrated as part of the organisational culture, behind which the dark triad can hide to pursue other selfish intentions. Depending on the organisation, such individuals may have a toxic and destructive impact of various levels of severity.

The options of intervention with such individuals are quite limited because they do not think there is a problem with their behaviour in the first case. This is why engaging with them in dialogical developmental techniques, such as counselling, therapy and coaching, for example, do not have high chances of success because they require the individual's participation in the process, coming from the belief that they need to change and that change would be good for them and others. This type of empathic awareness is lacking in those who present the traits of the dark triad.

And so the tension between threats to collective intentions presented by some individuals or our more generalised setbacks in clear judgement continue to be unresolved and may hold this unhelpful equilibrium for some time to come because evolution is rather slow.

Acknowledging this ambivalence and intervening as far as we can in the name of what has made us exceptional in our universe are important. Increasing overall self-awareness and self-development through a number of effective mechanisms, such as psychometric profiling, coaching, mentoring, counselling, therapy, team building, leadership and management development, with strong awareness of self, others and the wider context, can only enhance our collective emotional and social intelligence.

This in turn can enhance our ability for abstract, symbolic and scientific thinking, which balances our neurological activity of the brain with its instincts, genes and reflex triggers that support our very life but also give rise to the emergent upgrade represented by the gift of human mind.

SOCIETALCulture, leadership and people

The success of the human species is essentially based on the ability for abstract thinking alongside using social connectedness to amplify group cohesion and cultural accumulation. It is the combination of individual ingenuity and the critical mass of collective socially accumulated wisdom, knowledge and experience that together make for a greater and more successful outcome. The power of many is always a multiple of the power of one, in business and life.

In essence, what we constantly try to do by applying dedication and ingenuity is to create harmony by bringing together the activity of many into one fluid and consistent river of collective human contribution. A lot of research and many models and techniques have been developed to this end, and we are constantly designing and redesigning our approach to this fundamental need.

Perhaps applying the Pareto principles to the basics and getting the fundamentals right in our own actions may increase the yield of our investment of resources and energy and enable the rest of the more complex demands to follow.

SOCIETAL Culture: building a sense of belonging and shared meaning

Culture is about shared values and beliefs, collectively accepted norms and behaviours, symbols and artefacts that remind everyone and all those who belong to that wider group that they are in it together. Culture creates a sense of belonging and provides a strong sense of connectedness to those who belong to it.

The SOCIETAL acronym represents the words: S – safe, O – open, C – collaboration, I – innovation, E – ethics, T – technology, A – accountability and L – legacy and together create the fabric of the SOCIETAL Culture.

Safe is about working in a physical environment which is designed to offer good working conditions for people who spend at least seven or eight hours a day in offices. Safety is also about a psychological state where people feel that they can open up and discuss ideas and put forward suggestions without fear of being singled out, discriminated against or penalised in any way for being open, honest or enthusiastic. Physical and psychological safety in the workplace are basic factors that contribute to the happiness of those who pledged their skills and their experience to achieve enterprise purpose and objectives. Safety enables collaboration and innovation and is grounded in ethics.

Open represents the freedom of exchanging diverse ideas, being creative and innovative, combatting thinking biases and resistance to change and transformation. Openness enables communication across enterprise structure and hierarchies, honesty and ethical stance, allowing criticism and feedback from all individuals in the organisation without fear. Being open and openness is about legacy and accountability as well as ethics and collaboration.

Collaboration is an attitude and behaviour which values individual knowledge and contributions equally and invites and motivates the individuals in the enterprise to come together exchange and enhance their skills and create a body of knowledge that is greater than the sum of parts. It also enables an organisational structure which is flat, networked and capable of tapping into every individual well of capability to collectively generate new ways of working to achieve enterprise objectives and change the enterprise itself to a new adaptive state. Collaboration requires psychological safety and openness and results in technological advancements developed based on ethical principles.

Innovation is a key enterprise capability generated by contributions to solution-finding focussed creative thinking that translates into a new business product and services as well as new ways in which the organisation has to adapt to the dynamic internal and external forces – known and unknown, to design and redesign outcomes. This should benefit society, the planet and enterprise equally. Innovation is best achieved through openness and collaboration, leading to a legacy that is beneficial for future generations and the ecosystem.

Ethics represents the foundation of norms, moral values and actions that an enterprise follows in all its activities, whether they are internal in relation to their own people or external in relation to the wider society and the planet. Ethics should be part of the design at every step of product or service development, in the interaction between the people of the organisation and in the impact the enterprise has on all stakeholders involved in the supply and value chain, including the beneficiaries and users of their products and services. Ethics underpins innovation, collaboration and technological advancement, resulting in outputs that do not harm people and planet.

Technology is the ingredient that has become omnipresent as part of the civilisation of the 21st century and prevails in most activities undertaken by people in their private, public and working lives. Technology represents the way science is applied in the society with a view to benefit and increase the quality of life of the many. This is why technology has to be carefully developed and ethically used to avoid possible negative outcomes and remain a positive factor of the human civilisation rather than a hindrance or a threat. To improve the lives of many, it is necessary that technological advancement rest on ethical principles.

Accountability represents the responsibility that enterprises have for their behaviour in relation to the greater good, the wider society and their impact on natural resources and the planet. Businesses cannot endlessly exhaust irreplaceable resources and pollute the environment, and the best course of action is to avoid inflicting outrage on the world in the first instance by exercising ethics and implementing safety and innovation in the design of products and services and the overall relationship that the enterprise hast with society and nature. Accountability ensures that enterprises take their activity seriously and hold themselves responsible for failing ethics or reckless activity, should this arise. Accountability acts as a feedback mechanism and a reminder of the potential wide impact an enterprise can have on many people. Accountability, safety, openness and ethics are congruent and inter-related aspects of business processes.

Legacy is the consequence of the way organisations have taken responsibility for their impact on society considering at all times what they leave behind the future generations. Legacy is closely linked with accountability, technology, innovation and ethics and relates to the way irreplaceable resources are being utilised, alongside positive or negative outcome of their products or services, such as pollution, for example. Legacy requires enterprises to shift their gaze from the short-term impact and benefit and take responsibility and be accountable for the wider longer term consequences that they can trigger through their business activity.

The SOCIETAL acronym brings together the list of key values, beliefs, attitudes, aspirations and behaviours that together underpin the SOCIETALByDesign™ Culture. They are inter-related and interdependent and act together to support cohesion in enterprise dynamics and adaptation.

A SOCIETALCulture is intended and developed to be focussed on people – whether they are leaders or employees – and its process of evolution is based on flexible and agile change flowing both ways from the top down and from the grass roots up.

Resistance to change is the riskiest challenge of change programs, which determines if and how long it takes for change to take hold, the casualties on the way and the often unsuccessful completion of change programs in organisations.

But building a specific SOCIETALCulture in the first place can be done by leaders and other people working together to define, embody and act as one coherent entity, bring the SOCIETALByDesign™ Enterprise to life and working to fulfil its purpose by aligning everyone in thought and action to its mission, vision, values and outcomes.

SOCIETALLeaders: enablers of happiness and achievement at work

In line with its purpose and culture, SOCIETALLeaders will naturally embody attributes such as:

- Self-confidence, will enables them to collaborate with others without anxiety or a rivalry in relation to perceive diminishment of their role and status
- Intellectual openness to understand and benefit from the diversity of knowledge that various specialists can bring in for the benefit of business
- Collaboration and willingness to listening and use feedback as a constructive mechanism for improvement
- Being driven by intrinsic motivators rather than excessive financial gains and attributes of power
- Embracing selfless values and beliefs and include other in their considerations
- Staying even tempered and remain calm and constructive in time of success and celebration or challenge
- Finding meaning in enabling others to fulfil their potential and shine through contributions that they make to the organisation
- Distributing and delegating power and authority within the organisational network
- Respect and consideration for all levels and depths of contribution that each individual in the organisation makes
- Having the best interest of people within and outside the organisation at the forefront of their minds and reflect this through purpose, mission and vision, values and objectives
- Being able to consult and accept different ideas and flexibly modify their own views in light of new knowledge, experience and information coming from personal, individual and collective sources

SOCIETALLeaders understand how business and society are closely linked through the same people and that what business does impacts society just as what society does impacts business. This enables the SOCIETALLeadership to connect with SOCIETALPeople and work together thought feedback loops to control that which can be controlled directly (e.g. the work environment) and influence that which cannot be directly controlled (e.g. government policy) and finally by building the capability of resilience when facing uncontrolled internal or external factors.

Looking back to a succession of jobs that took me across decades of career, I reflected on my own leadership experiences with managers and teams.

RICHARD

A visionary maverick, charismatic, articulate, authentic and enthusiastic, Richard inspired and motivated everyone around him, paying attention to enable people to be at their best by providing tools, training and recognition to all in his very large team. At the same time, he also defended our collective interests, further up, when he fought for and obtained good budgets to always have best infrastructure and good pay for his department. I am sure that, as our champion, he may have also been a bit of a challenge to his own less visionary board colleagues!

DANIEL

Mild mannered, quietly spoken, even tempered, Daniel was the enabler of his team's individual capabilities. He was always available in the background, spoke, looked and behaved like one of the team and deferred to the specific knowledge that we each had and managed to always be out of the way, whilst always there and present when we needed him. He was a quietly reassuring facilitator of excellence and always kept us informed of the conversations that were happening above our station in the company hierarchies. He encouraged cross-training and peer learning in the team and collaboration between colleagues and made sure that everyone of us knew of the strengths and talents of the others in the team.

MARIE

A direct and open communicator, Marie's behaviour didn't change whether she spoke to her subordinates, peers or superiors. She demonstrated great confidence and trust even in new recruits who may have had little previous experience. She was always reassuring and ready to show or do herself what needed to be done for others to learn. She was elegant and graceful in manner, whilst equally clear about the high standards she expected. She always praised and admired the talents of others and quite openly acknowledged her own weaknesses and strengths.

ROBERT

A towering presence, Robert was honest and competent, with excellent intuition for people and business, infinite patience and calm, a reassuring voice. He treated everyone with care and fairness, making judgements according to the qualities of the person in front of him. A natural mentor, he invested time and patience in those he worked with, his reassuring supporting presence always made every one of us feel that we did make a contribution and held our professional station even when in fact we were still just learning. His trust, generosity and patience in supporting and nurturing our own aspirations and desire to do well were exceptionally reassuring and empowering.

ALEX

Very bright and always present in the moment, Alex was interested in the people in his team as whole individuals and not just specialists in their domain. He readily and consistently acknowledged everyone's expertise and was not afraid to call in and collaborate with people who knew certain aspects of business better than him. He also acknowledged other people's strengths publicly and deferred to those who knew something different or better than him without reservation. He was open, polite and quietly spoken, whilst clearly demanding and

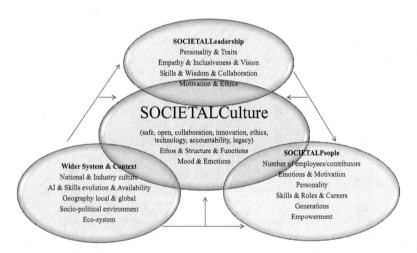

Figure 3.2 SOCIETALCulture = Leader + People + Wider context

Note: AI = artificial intelligence

driving business objectives to high standards. The interactions with him were always rich in context and felt like a dialogue between two human beings rather than a narrow exchange of specific technical knowledge and complementary areas of specialisms.

Reflecting on these examples, I was intrigued by the fact that these individuals could not have been more different from each other, and gathering them all in one room would have created the most diverse group one could imagine. Yet they all shared in the same spirit of SOCIETAL attributes.

All these exceptional leaders embodied the "magic recipe" – which for most businesses large and small continues to remain to this day and for some time to come – that aspirational level of mastery in enabling people at work to flourish.

SOCIETALPeople: custodians of culture and leader makers

The change and evolution of the SOCIETALCulture starts from a different place to begin with and requires SOCIETALLeaders to accept change from the grass roots up and work with the mood, personalities, aspirations, needs and expectations of the people who are the heart of the enterprise, which reflect society at large.

SOCIETALPeople that will thrive in SOCIETALCultures are likely to be:

- Pursuing self-development and self-actualisation in the company of others
- Driven by intrinsic motivators and values and beliefs which reflect an appreciation of achievements, collaboration, excellence and enjoyment of expressing their skills and capabilities through chosen work activities
- Curious, enjoy change and have an appetite to continuously develop professionally and personally by acquisition of new skills, training and development opportunities
- Show openness and willingness to take direction as well as the direction in line with circumstances and levels of expertise that are required in specific business settings
- Care about people in general and how poor values and beliefs that protects humanistic values and the distribution of advantages and opportunities to many instead of just a few
- Have confidence and an ability to find meaning and purpose in what they do, rather than wait for reassurance from others, to sustain their self belief whilst exercising their roles

- Be self-directed, self-sufficient and able to effectively operate in their own right as well as in collaboration with others
- Built for themselves a life of achievement through knowledge, wisdom, respect of self and others, enjoyment of people and society and an aspiration to leave behind a positive constructive legacy as opposed to focus on materialistic symbols of status and power that deprive others to provide for one's own egotistic desires

The culture and leadership of any organisation enable an environment where individuals manifest themselves within the connections, relationships and exchanges that they experience with each other, a process which picks up and transforms personal contributions and identities into an outcome which is greater than the sum of parts.

But if that outcome is something not most or all members of the organisation believe in, self-interest and ruthless ambition in one person or influential group may distort and derail the direction of the business as a whole.

In a SOCIETALByDesign™ organisation, there is alignment among culture, leadership and people, and together they direct, form and transform each other in an inter-dependent co-created system. Feedback loops inform and correct the dynamic of the enterprise, and whilst maintaining a firm sight on its purpose, they may also have to design and re-deigns the ways to get there in response to factors of change from within and the outer environment.

The resulting cohesion stems out of resilience and the shared beliefs that hold the people on course in a shared journey they constantly map and re-map together.

Acknowledging emotions as fractals of human nature
and testing positive emotional resonance

The SOCIETALByDesign™ Model of design and development of adaptive agile enterprises places emotions at the heart of management responsibility because of their tremendous direct and indirect impact on business success.

In fact, politics and business have always known this and have handsomely benefited from emotional manipulation with outcomes both ways. Dictators have taken entire nations to destruction, whilst democratic leaders have inspired nations to victory. Some businesses have managed to addict people to legally available drugs, whilst other have started entire movements for fitness. Everything from advertising campaigns to political campaigns and election outcomes ride on the emotional waves that underpin, often unconsciously, our choices and actions. Those who know how to ride this wave, understand its power and use its energy have won many advantages, often to the detriment of many others.

The financial value of emotions tactically used for gain by politics and business has been proven a very long time ago. So why is it not a key part of management science and daily management and practice everywhere? And instead, all those who talk about "heart" in business are often apologetic about bringing such topic into leadership, management and C-suite conversations. Could this be because of influences from the wider social system, for example, cultural practices and gender dynamics, in which some nations are more expressive of emotions than others or men are expected to be less emotional than women, alongside the gender balance and dynamics in the workplace and in senior positions that are typically occupied by men?

Whatever the explanation – which is undoubtedly subtle and complex – both men and women in all cultures know how to manipulate emotions and do so on "as-needed" basis.

With so much known about the advantage of opportunistically involving emotions, it is just a matter of choice and policy to actually introduce emotions as a normal item on the business management agenda.

We are the result of biological, psychological, sociological and philosophical imperatives, and all these complex forces play their hand, whether we know it or not and whether we like it or not. Our life force comes from our biological foundation, and we are born with complex and sophisticated adaptive mechanisms that take care of us and ensure our survival. An important part of this fundamental capability is provided by our emotions, which act as a fuel that energises our thoughts and actions.

But emotions are one of those challenging domains in which we are set back by the fact that they are embodied in our physiology whilst also in some way connected to our thoughts and cognition. We are not quite sure how this happens whilst the boundaries in the hierarchies between shear physical sensation and complex thoughts and feelings is really blurred and entangled.

The impact of emotions can be seen everywhere, everyday around us, particularly when they flare up and express in actions that range from small gestures to extreme and extravagant displays of the most varied kind, from abject to sublime.

The fact is that in many cultures or socio-economic settings, people do not like to talk about emotions, and in business, conversations about emotions and feelings are considered "soft and fluffy". Business language has no place for "touchy feely" talk because it runs the show and solves its problems based on hard facts, evidence and by use of clear models, tools and methods.

Yet keeping in mind that emotions are strongly embodied and translate into chemical and electrical activity – that can be measured – we would be best advised to pay attention because there is nothing "fluffy" about our genes and the activity of our systems.

Biology is blunt, intractable, purposeful and entrenched. Biology is a formidable force which typically wins most of the time if opposed. When biology takes hold of us, we become powerless, and a huge amount of effort, energy and will need to be deployed to moderate biological and genetic triggers or reflex actions and impulses.

Emotions are formidable manifestations of biology, and it is incomprehensible that business and society at large – also tasked with providing order and structure to collective lives and activities – are resistant to acknowledge and face the formidable force of emotions and accept it as a critical business factor. The conversation about emotions is necessary because, frankly, talking about emotions by far outweighs our current ability to also act in relation to them and actually walk that talk.

Emotions are an outcome of biology and nature and lend themselves to an analogy with fractals, both being considered here as aspects of dialectic and complex systems dynamics. Fractals are irregular shapes or structures found in nature, in which any part chosen to be considered is in fact similar in shape to a given larger or smaller part. There are fractals we are familiar with in nature. We not only see them but also eat some of them even if we do not know them by this name; examples include sea shells, pinecone seeds, pineapples, broccoli heads, sea stars and urchins, water droplets, leaves, ice crystals, trees, air bubbles, snowflakes, fern, thunder, peacock, shorelines, rivers and fiords, stalactite and stalagmites.

They create complex pattern every time they self-repeat but remain self-similar when scaling up or down even whilst generating very different and irregular but much more complex outcomes. For example, a stone at the base of a foothill is a miniature resembling the hill is came from and remains self-similar when scaled up and seen as a mountain or scaled down to be seen as a pebble.

Whilst modelling fractals is done with idealised perfect shapes, in reality, fractals have varying degrees of roughness and a character which indicates the way they occur in nature and not in human modelling. Fractals also illustrate the path from simple to complex because they are repeatable, never-ending patterns. As such, they form objects for sciences of geometry, mathematics and chaos theory, fundamentally trying to find consistency and some order in the amazing and dynamic universe of trees, clouds, mountains, cups of coffee, dollops of cream and – why not? – human emotions. After all, biometrics and their processing by artificial intelligence and algorithms are precisely an example of the way digitised computer science attempts to captures and order reality, nature and life itself.

In the SOCIETALByDesign™ Model, fractals are analogies for emotions which fit at the foundation of something much more complex which emerges from repetition of certain patterns.

Emotional fractals of anger, sadness, disgust and fears, if repeated over and over and over again, will develop into feelings, attitudes, aspirations, values and beliefs and eventually express in communication and behaviour, which all carry the original negative essence amplified many times, leading to a highly likely negative outcomes of all shades, all the way to sheer destruction of self and others. Anger as a fractal emotion, is self-similar but if scaled up or down over time, can change into something completely different.

The positive emotional fractals of joy, love, happiness, trust and connectedness, if repeated many times, over will also give rise to a different set of feelings, attitudes, aspirations, values, beliefs, thoughts, words and actions, which become the foundation of all the shades between kindness and achievement to extraordinary quantum leaps that can move the entire civilisation forward.

Our duty towards our emotional fractals is to embed and maintain those that lead to positive outcomes and derail the others that take us straight into the dark side of human nature. This can be done by our own work of self-development, when we grow and develop the ability to make judgements and exercise will, but it is also in the hands of the society and the people around us, who enable that development starting with parents and carers, friends and colleagues, in the settings of our personal lives and education and work settings.

The SOCIETALByDesign™ Enterprise acknowledges the importance that the environment has in generating and maintaining positive emotions and by exercising its purpose of looking after people and developing their full potential is effectively creating an environment for the innovative and creative side of human nature to flourish, whilst mitigating through enterprise policies and instruments the potential proliferation of negative emotional fractals.

There is nothing more powerful in both constructive and destructive outcomes than what comes out of love, joy, enthusiasm, happiness

Table 3.2 SOCIETALByDesign™ framework, ethos and underlying positive emotions

DESIGN ANDRE-DESIGN *Adaptive Helical Iterations* *ART > Science*	*KNOWLEDGE* *Multidisciplines* *Cross-functions* *Art + Science + Technology*	*DEVELOPMENT* *Adaptive Helical Iteration* *SCIENCE > Art*
I. SPARK	WE CAN W – wisdom E – energy C – collective capability A – alignment N – networked	I. TRIGGER
II. IMMERSION	EMPOWER E – empathy M – motivation P – purpose O – organisation W – wellness E – emotions R – recognition And be	II. ENQUIRY
III. ENVISIONING	SOCIETAL S – safe O – open C – collaboration I – innovation E – ethics T – technology A – accountability L – legacy	III. CONFIGURING
IV. REALISING	to go FAR F – flexibility A – agility R – resilience	IV. DEPLOYMENT

or hate, anger, greed, envy and indifference, to underpin people's best and worst behaviours, individually and collectively.

The SOCIETALByDesign™ Model is about people in business and in the wider society, and it is for people and therefore naturally suited to overlay emotions and people's unconscious triggers on its framework through the people-related science that sits in between design and development and into business practice.

Therefore, it is possible to position within the frame presented earlier a number of emotional resonance tests that relate to the various stages of design and development but also across any and all activities that an enterprise may undertake, including helical iterations.

"WE CAN EMPOWER and be SOCIETAL to go FAR": ethos and emotions

This SOCIETALByDesign™ Ethos brings together the notions of emotions and other invisible drivers such as aspirations, values and attitudes that support behaviours and desired outcomes as the way to bring cohesion to enterprise working life through its culture.

The words chosen represent emotions but also aspirations or attitudes that are buoyed by a positive energy charge and can be easily used as check lists around any and all activities exercised in business and in managed or peer settings, by any members of the organisation.

The Ethos is also a reminder of the SOCIETALCulture agenda to:

- Demonstrate the way we do things around here (the how).
- Clearly articulate what we care about (the why).
- Provide respectful status for all in the group (the who).
- Take responsibility for outcomes and long term legacy of our actions (the when).

To maintain the agenda of the desired culture for the SOCIETAL-ByDesign™ Enterprise, there must be in place open doors and feedback mechanisms that enable whistle blowing, escalation, critique, criticism and suggestions for improvements to travel through internal channels of communication around the vertical and horizontal structures and collaborative networks to those who have power of decision or influence.

Having such opportunity for feedback in place decreases the chance of toxicity taking hold of the organisation and spilling outside into wider society, as well as the possibility of maintaining the SOCIETAL-ByDesign™ Enterprise's ethical and purposeful integrity when and if surrounded by a toxic wider environment.

If the enterprise is aligned around the purpose of looking after people inside and outside, such policy and practice should translate into everyday business as usual and contain potential internal and external negative currents – which are part of normal events of business and social life – from rising up and taking hold of a majority of the organisation.

The SOCIETALByDesign™ organisation respects those who can shine a light on things that others may not see and will diminish thinking biases, be it individual or collective, of the people in the enterprise.

It may be that within the diversity of an organisations pool of talent, it is those who sit outside the majority who might have a novel and unique perspective on things, and therefore their voice, although in minority, should count as much as everyone else's.

- WE CAN – an acronym for wisdom, energy, collective capability, alignment and networks – captures the idea that where there is collective positive energy, there is the knowledge and a way forward, co-created by the alignment of the group
- EMPOWER – stands for empathy, motivation, purpose, organisation, workmanship, emotions and recognition – capturing the notion that emotion and motivation support the achievement of an empathic purpose, through recognised workmanship of the organisation
- SOCIETAL- stands for safe, open, collaborative, innovative, ethics, technology, accountability and legacy – capturing the philosophy of the enterprise that values safety, openness and collaboration for its people and uses innovation and technology to create an ethical legacy for which it stands accountable
- FAR – flexibility, agility, resilience – highlights that evolution and adaptation are complex processes which involve not only agility but also flexibility to recover and benefit from stability and consolidation, between iterations of change, and do so with the energy of hope and belief in a better future that come from resilience

These words and acronyms can be used to "test emotional resonance" in a way that may appear simple, but it is not. They are positioned as an easy way to remind ourselves and specifically to remind managers and leaders that we need to ensure happiness at work as a key ingredient in the recipe for success. We have to keep close watch on the emotional states of the people at work, show interest and care, and most important, use such observations to change the prevailing emotions in the dynamic of the interaction, aiming to maintain emotional positivity in individuals and teams.

Stating that happy people work well and make customers and society happy needs no research results (although available if required) to be proven correct, and we know this from social wisdom and common sense, too. The interconnected world of emotions, attitudes and aspirations are like human fractals, quite individual and precisely outlined but yet giving rise, by repetition to intricate and amazingly endless patterns that in reality are rough and unique, creating an all-encompassing tapestry, delicate yet incredibly strong and quite resilient to pressures.

Emotional fractals are created and embedded in practice and by repetition, and it is best that we entrust the fabrication of this bio-chemo-electrical lace to positive factors that repeat and amplify that take us away from the dark and into the bright side of human potential. Individually and collectively, we do have the option to influence outcomes, so let us use it responsibly and wisely.

Monitoring what we want to improve

All human activity is underpinned by pragmatism because it results in an outcome that is necessary or desired at the outset, consciously or unconsciously – except for play, in which no pragmatic objective is set as a specified outcome. Businesses are commercial activities exercised as an essential part of human exchange and are set up with a pragmatic outcome in mind. Therefore, they also need mechanisms to verify if the activity taking place is as planned, and usually such indicators are chosen or devised to fit the needs of measurements and quantification, which are useful to the specifics of each function or business.

There are three indicators positioned in the model, as being key top level and specific for the SOCIETALByDesign™ enterprise:

1 The key enterprise capability indicator (KECI)
2 The key enterprise adaptability indicator (KEAI)
3 The key enterprise happiness indicator (KEHI)

1 Capability

Enterprise capability is positioned as the key indicator of success and defined as the ability and capacity of a business to deploy what is necessary, to effectively achieve the objectives that it has set for itself.

Unlike competencies, capability is a more evolved holistic perspective that takes into consideration individuality and diversity of a person, having a holistic approach to tasks and relations as a source of good performance, appreciating individual knowledge, experience and meaning making as attributes for future success, valuing and being curious about a person's richness of knowledge and developed self, holding a contextual and systemic perspective in personal and professional interactions. The suitability of the capability approach to our complex, unpredictable and volatile times is self-evident.

Optimum overall capability enables the business to maintain the point of equilibrium whereby it is comfortably cruising with all necessary resources and assets deployed through balanced, flexible, fit and effective business processes.

Capability sits between acquisition and development of all the necessary elements (e.g. talent, technology, leadership) on the one hand and attrition, divestment or loss of such necessary elements on the other.

Acquisition may either provide what is necessary (e.g. skills, technology, leadership) and be ready to deploy and support the required level of capability as soon as possible or can bring in resources with potential strengths and advantages that will need some time to be developed to achieve the full efficiency level, which will then fully support capability and be deployed into enterprise dynamics to keep it running at the intended and necessary level.

SOCIETALByDesign™ Enterprise Capability can be seen as the point of perfect equilibrium of the mid-day sun, which sits between sunrise (replenishment by creation of new products and services) and sunset (divestment of previous versions of output or activities no longer useful).

Enterprise capability is the critical business indicator that needs to be constantly monitored to trigger ether replenishment or divestment of what is necessary for an effective enterprise life.

Human talent is a singular and most risky factor of enterprise capability and its success. Because of the dynamic movement of human talent in organisations, some of which is planned and predictable and some of which is not, organisational capability is the point of equilibrium which is constantly threatened by forces from within and outside the organisation, particularly when it come to the human factor.

Human talent is one of the key necessary elements of success usually referred to in increasing degrees of complexity:

- from skills, defined as the ability to do a particular task or work well
- to competencies, which are observable sets of knowledge made of several elements such as skills, abilities and personal attributes, leading to effective and enhanced performance
- to capabilities, defined as the intersection of ability and capacity with the added value that it also reflects a higher level of judgment of complex situations with a perspective on time and use of intuition, maturity and wisdom in the pursuit of outcomes that may be distanced in the future and subject to non-linear causality and results.

Human talent is itself a dynamic force that varies between points of replenishment and points of attrition.

Internally, the acquisition of potential has to maintain equilibrium, for example, between new resources that require some time to develop o be deployed at its full actual capability into the organisation and resources that are attracted to the organisation and are fully developed and ready to be deployed at full capability. At the other end, it is necessary to monitor the process of attrition and the mix among planned retirements, people leaving the organisation of their own accord but unexpectedly and talent that has to be promoted, restructured, retrained or redeployed because of the evolving technology and business process efficiencies.

Externally, the advancement of new technologies and ways of working constantly gives rise to new jobs, professions and career paths alongside an initial shortage of highly desirable skills, competencies and capabilities that accompany such changes on an ongoing basis. This external pressure places the enterprise in a competitive state in which it needs to fight for the right talent and promote its brand and advantages of joining to attract the right but limited number of people that are equally sought after by competitors in the industry.

In a SOCIETALByDesign™ Enterprise, capability also develops with maturity. In other words, within its own effective parameters, capability can vary between a moment when the sum total of what is necessary is deployed and is fully functional but not necessarily 100% effective and which by maturing transform potential into actual and acquire an edge of efficiency and effectiveness that is almost 100%. And this transformation is carefully monitored and managed as a critical principle.

Whilst the key enterprise capability indicator is essential to a SOCIETALByDesign™ Enterprise, it is a composite of and closely connected with other key indicators that are chosen and specific to each enterprise; and ideally capability and outcomes should match. At the same time, both success and capability indicators are informed by gaps in specific key indicators, which will flag needs for development, acquisition or divestment of talent.

The KECI is a dynamic measure and composite measure that draws its information from different sources. These sources sample and collect information at different points in the talent, technology, processes, and structural lifecycles that have to be in synch in an ongoing and dynamic manner.

Six factors of the KECI are:

1   Ethics and purpose-led management and leadership
2   Agile and flexible management of the enterprise structure and its talent

3   Collaborative, innovative and adaptive culture
4   Enabling workplace infrastructure, functions, policies and pro-
     cesses which support business success, safety and wellness of
     people inside and outside of the enterprise (employees, collabo-
     rators, clients and society)
5   Acknowledging human thinking biases, the dark side of human
     nature and maladaptive personalities, which can all impact the
     entire enterprise and having mitigating mechanisms in place
6   Multidisciplinary and cross-functional resources and poly-
     maths, leading a human–machine synergy and adoption of
     technology that is sustainable and does not harm society or the
     environment.

Because human talent is positioned as the greatest risk and success
factor in the SOCIETALByDesign™ enterprise, it is important to briefly
cover two aspects regarding the actual quality of talent.

With competencies required in the future such as higher thinking
and cognitive functions, dealing with uncertainty and complexity,
adapting to ongoing change and innovation, alongside forging collaborations across domains, the future is getting neither simpler nor
clearer, and it may be some time before things settle in the new post–
Fourth Industrial Revolution equilibrium.

In light of future changes, the quality of resources needed for the
success of the SOCIETALByDesign™ enterprise must include polymaths and people with expertise in social sciences and philosophy.

Polymaths – mandatory talent for a SOCIETALByDesign™ Enterprise

Polymaths, "jacks of all trades and masters of . . . all," actually enjoy
a formal definition. A polymath is a person whose expertise spans a
number of different subject areas; such a person is known to draw on
complex bodies of knowledge to solve specific problems. A polymath
is a thinker who is highly competent in several fields of science and
the arts and embodies the principle that people should not limit their
capacity and should embrace all knowledge and develop their capabilities as fully and widely as possible.

A polymath is a competent "tree watcher" who does not lose sight
of the "woods". A polymath is capable of seeing the deeper connections between sciences and apparently different areas of specialism,
find underlying common denominators and "stack" apparently disjointed disciplines to open up amazing possibilities for cross transfer

and cross-fertilisation of methodologies and solutions that eventually lead to invention, innovation and overall knowledge advancement. Western positivism has pushed specialisation to such an extreme that integration of fragmented and disjointed aspects of the same reality and object of study has become a scarce capability, not entertained even in speculation. But only a few hundred years ago, around the world and the Europe of the Renaissance, individuals were encouraged to be well rounded and capable of excelling in as many domains as possible.

Before that, in antiquity, educated people were also knowledgeable in more areas than one and able to make, as such, a wider range of contributions. Philosophy, initially the science of all sciences, went hand in hand with mathematics, astronomy, chemistry and natural science. The same expectation applied to crafts and arts.

But now, the tide is turning again, and we see increasingly an acceptance and appreciation of "generalists" (who contribution across domains, on a higher integrative level), alongside polymaths who are multispecialists and have in fact never ceased to be the pioneers of innovation and significant change in science and technology.

Welcoming such talent into the SOCIETALByDesign™ Enterprise requires adequate recruitment processes and a complete renewal of the way people generally "label" others with an immovable demand for explicit clarity which greatly diminishes the value of those who can offer more than one thing at a time.

Recruiters and employers are quite risk averse and tend to hire for "safety", meaning there has to be a clear label on one's skills and the person must have done in recent times, and consistently, that which is "written on the tin". What this means is that polymaths cannot honestly communicate to the market: "I am good at a number of things and can do more than one job" even if this is true. They are forced to diminish themselves and hide their true potential, a process which is not only disrespectful and humiliating but also a huge loss of talent for potential employers.

This is why SOCIETALByDesign™ Enterprises actively look for and welcome such "professional oddities" because innovation and technological advancement today as well as the birth of new hybrid sciences and technologies only demonstrate that multidisciplinary and cross-functional collaborations are the only way to find solutions to increasingly complex needs and problems, and such mixed polymath capabilities are mandatory going forward if we are to adapt to the volatile, unpredictable and complex digital world of tomorrow.

Psychologist and social science professionals – mandatory
talent for a SOCIETALByDesign™ Enterprise

In conventional enterprises, accountants keep a cold eye on the bottom line and constantly adjust figures, looking at possibilities of making more profit, which may well include reduction of posts, employee benefits, perks and advantages or anything else that is considered non-essential in the collection and transformation of skills and work hours into profit. Because of this, they can easily, at the stroke of a pen, change the quality of life of hundreds of people employed by the company and never really have any personal or human contact.

Business managers are tasked with the pursuit of individual objectives, but many managers are in management posts by chance. An accidental manager is a person who has proven outstanding technical skills and is promoted because of those achievements, through hierarchies or functional groups, to a post in which they need to look after teams of people. Many land this next level of responsibility without the soft skills which are not related to their core technical skills Soft skills include communication, motivation, relationship building, empathy and listening. They may lack the even more sophisticated knowledge of individual differences, personality styles and team dynamics, all necessary for a professionally trained manager to use in the practice of people management.

Business leaders are equally challenged, and as we know from the endless leadership programs that are being proposed and rolled out across businesses, achieving high leadership capabilities remains a moving target not only because leadership is such a complex capability but also because the requirements of a leader keep changing from decade to decade in line with the technological advancement, the structures and ways of working in organisations and the wider society.

As a result, in conventional businesses, the accountants, managers and leaders at the helm of enterprises are all capable of delivering some of the requirements of those positions but not others. All these roles contain a core of technical knowledge – which they often have – alongside another set of skills that belong to other disciplines, related to people and the understanding of the human nature and the complex and holistic environment and life of employees, as individuals responsible not only for themselves but also their dependents, further influencing or contributing to friends and the wider society – which they seldom, if ever, have.

But the SOCIETALByDesign™ Enterprises are centred on people inside and outside the company by way of its very purpose. So management practice must align and deliver with expertise pertaining to the social sciences of psychology, sociology, anthropology, evolutionary psychology, behavioural psychology and neuroscience.

Therefore, the specific and mandatory expertise that the SOCIETAL-ByDesign™ Enterprises have to have as part of multidisciplinary or cross-functional teams and collaborations is that of specialists or polymaths, competent in psychology and social sciences alongside business management and administration.

The employment of psychologists, sociologists and behavioural scientists in SOCIETALByDesign™ Enterprises as permanent full-time or part-time members of management and leadership teams and roles is self-evident if we really want to end once and for all chasing the tale of never-ending management and leadership "quick fix" training and development that continue to fail the necessary level of soft skills capability, which are core expertise for other professionals and domains of science, which are not sufficiently used by business in a collaborative manner.

2 *Adaptability*

Enterprise adaptability is positioned as a key ability of an enterprise to evolve and respond to internal and external forces by adapting to find a new point of equilibrium for balanced and successful functionality and continued achievement of its purpose and objectives.

Adaptability is also a composite indicator that measures the combined effect of three dynamic factors:

1   Flexibility: as a measure of being able to move between a state of equilibrium and a phase of change, without breaking; being pliable, changing without breaking, coping with change – embracing the "third option" of motion and stability
2   Agility: as a measure of being able to exercise speed and equilibrium, being fast, balanced, whilst in motion – embracing the option of motion
3   Resilience: as a measure of being able to recover and consolidate, bounce back to a functional stable state, learn from experience, remain positive and hopeful – embracing the option of firm stability

Flexibility, agility and resilience together manifest in the dynamics of enterprise adaptability by bringing together design, development, redesign and transformation in light of internal and external pressures, including fresh sources of knowledge, helpful in solution devising. Together they provide outcomes such as:

- The ability to identify new opportunities, move on and rebuild
- Transferring and repurposing capabilities and competencies by innovation
- Resilience to never give up and just pursue the collective vision of a possible good future
- Remaining empathetic and considerate of ourselves and others even when going through difficulties
- Tremendous resourcefulness and the energy to bounce back after difficult times
- Nurturing hope as a positive force for renewal, at times of destruction even when individual and collective world are shaken by disruptions
- Power to recover and return to an even stronger identity after adversity.

3 Happiness

The definition of happiness is not easy because happiness is a multi-fold construct. But an attempted definition would include the experience of positive emotions such as pleasure and joy often in the here and now alongside an evaluation of a good quality of life and the subjective enjoyment of well-being that bring together the sense that one's life is meaningful and worthwhile.

Essentially, happiness combines emotions with cognition but also with activity and expression of one's individual qualities and attributes in the exercise of something meaningful. Happiness therefore combines a subjective experiential and reflective aspect together becoming manifest through actual engaged activity in which skill and challenge are finely balanced in a dynamic interaction. In our context, happiness is understood to mean flourishing in a work-related environment in the company of others.

The study of happiness at work has produced the concept of "flow", which is described as a state in which people are involved in something meaningful and stretching, that uses and challenges their skills and when one loses the sense of time and place, completely absorbed in the activity that is pursued in a controlled manner and for the sake of achieving mastery of the task, in an effort that brings joy.

Flow can be achieved in any activity from music to sports and science and across genders, classes, ages and cultures. Flow involves concentration on the task, clarity of goals and reward, an experience of effortlessness with a sense of intrinsic activity reward. Challenge, skills and actions are merged and aligned, and there is feeling of control over the task. In popular language, this is also known as "being in the zone".

The enemies of flow are boredom, apathy and worry, whilst anxiety and relaxation are both passive states that do not induce activity. Optimum enablers of flow are arousal, which engages activity and control in which the sense of "I can" is also engaged.

In the SOCIETALByDesign™ Model, happiness depends on and can be assessed by three factors:

• Physical and mental well-being and workplace safety – which eliminate anxiety, worries, boredom and apathy
• Inclusiveness and equal opportunity to flourish professionally (developing skills and career progression with meaningful work) – which enhance career paths and individual choices to professionally evolve
• Internal structures that allow for autonomy, collaboration and participation – which provide goals, challenges, and an environment to enjoy working with others

Helical iterations and agile adaptive transformation

Our existence as humans has always been marked by the need to relate and adapt to our environment. In the beginning, it was mainly the natural environment, where life was precarious and difficult and every day brought with it the unexpected success or failure in the pursuit of survival. Providing food involved daily effort and an unpredictable chance for success. Life in cold and dark caves was not easy even if caves provided shelter from the elements.

The development of tools and the ability of humans to adapt and evolve, create communities, engage in agriculture, domesticate animals and organise in rural settlements enabled further developments in exchange of goods and ideas that became over time increasingly more sophisticated. Gone was the need to chase calories on a daily basis. The food was now available pretty much next to the tables, and as time went by, life became much easier.

Humans initiated and have maintained to this day their ability to benefit from social cultural accumulation, which enables each generation to benefit from the progress of the generations that have come before.

Social accumulation is how industrial revolutions have been key engines in spreading scientific discoveries and the artefacts of human intelligence, through technology, to a large number of individuals and society in general. A parallel human-made environment now marks the planet layered over the natural landscape.

Human society today is a far cry from the original human groups living in caves and crude shelters. Along with the sophistication of our human societies came our increasing demands and aspirations to satisfy these basic needs such as food, shelter, clothing, health and social interaction.

We also have needs to express our thoughts through symbolic, artistic and aesthetic representations, documenting collective experiences that bound us together, celebrations of events that marked our personal history and our individual expressions. All contributions to the bigger legacy left by successive generations and adding to it for the civilisation of generations to come.

Each generation seeks to find answers to the same fundamentally human questions. This is why stating that every design is a redesign and every new solution is fundamentally answering the same old problems is pertinent to our view on the evolution of society, business and enterprise activity.

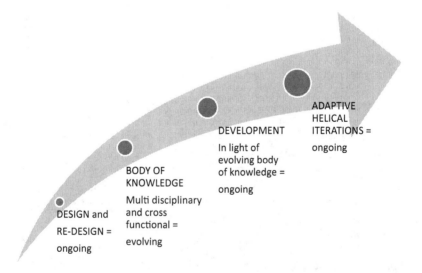

Figure 3.3 Adaptive evolution leading to helical iterations in SOCIETALBy-Design™ Enterprises

Evolution involves adaptation and therefore allows for multidirectional movements and changes. The starting point for each iteration is a new state of equilibrium, and the next loop of the spiral can then take an enterprise from simple to complex but also back to simple in a new form, with new purpose, connections to the outside systems and a new internal configuration, possibly simpler than before but enabling greater adaptive stability and a new state of equilibrium. In this case, evolution is by a change to superior functionality enabled by a simpler structure or narrower scope, with new connecting relationships between internal parts of the system and with the external players, as a result of its history and related adaptive options available at a point in time.

The ongoing dynamics of helical design, re-design and adaptive development

Helical iterations represent intended movements between stages and levels of development, driven by intended design and development cycles and by use of selected multidisciplinary cross-functional bodies of knowledge. These cycles initiate changes at points in time, reflecting and responding to known or surprise factors and forces, within or outside the enterprise system.

Influencing factors and their related responses may originate anywhere and have any scope of impact from enterprise system specific to outer systems such as society or nature. Outcomes of such design and development influencing dynamics range from changes of one enterprise process in up to 3 months, to develop, change and improve a functional systems in 2–5 years or to develop, change and improve multiple value chains of a company over 20–25 years.

The activity and evolution of enterprises may in turn cause intended and unintended consequences of any magnitude in the outer social and natural systems.

Causality and outcomes are co-located within human agency, activity, reactions and feedback loops and therefore present characteristics of "wicked problems" in which inputs and outputs are only partly transparent. The work-related human contributors to enterprise life and activity act as conduits and interfaces between enterprise systems and subsystems and the rest of non–work-related human activity.

The very nature, complexity, variability and activity of people inside and outside work generate the need for continuous and dynamic enterprise adjustments and re-adjustments by design, re-design, ongoing development and review of means. This re-design is based on new knowledge or re-evaluation and re-mixing of exiting bodies of knowledge from science and practice. Human presence and its unpredictability introduce permeability, vulnerability and risk within and across systems. This is why the work of running enterprises in the way intended, is an ongoing work, even when the purpose is to maintain the status quo. Limited or lack of control over a multitude of factors, including those embodied by people extends beyond the breached enterprise boundaries into socio-political, natural and outer space settings and events, making constant cycles of adjustments necessary.

Such iterations can take an enterprise from small and simple to complex and large structures and back the other way but always circling around the permanent core of an enterprise's legacy, which reflects its history and accumulated wisdom and learnings within the wider context of society, technology and human civilisation.

Steam power, engines, electricity, electronics, information technology, and since the cluster of innovations of the 1980s, digital technologies, have all created opportunities for movement of people, goods and ideas, like never before.

The interaction of human beings has now extended beyond the cave, the village, the town, the county, the nation or the continent, all the way to a live and globalised expanse, with its own unpredictable 24/7 dynamics. The world, just like the life of an enterprise, is never at rest, never sleeps, is constantly forming, constantly transforming and forever emerging.

Concluding with hope and confidence: using what we know to prepare for the unknown

The successive steam, electricity, electronics and digital revolutions have created technologies which combined have completely change the life on our planet. Science and technology have placed at our disposal applications which have generated the tremendous abundance in what we can do to improve the quality of our lives well beyond our basic needs into the outer realms of our wants, fantasies, dreams and desires.

The Internet; the smart phone, which is effectively a pocket computer; e-commerce; the rise of service industries; the automation and sophistication of manufacturing and supply chain; the importance and utilisation of data in all human-related activities; the global reach and power established by technology platform providers; the use of advertising and financial speculations to generate profits; social media; and the globalised exchange of goods, services and ideas, taking place all the time in real time, have changed not only our tangible world but also our internalised experiences and mental representations of the world.

New values, beliefs, attitudes and aspirations have given rise to social memes, fads, fashions and behaviours in private, public and work-related environments, never seen before. Today they sit alongside previously accumulated and established values, beliefs and behaviours that may be hundreds of years old. The world has always changed and transformed, and again at the dawn of the 21st century, our human civilisation is going through yet another transition and transformation, finding itself on the edge of chaos, between the forces of the past and the drivers of the future.

The tremendous technological advancements of the past 50 years have brought with them tremendous benefits, which at times have been shared and distributed amongst large numbers of people. At the same time, the overconfidence in our collective power and achievements and an obsession with continuous growth, ongoing profitability and unbounded consumption have together created the dark shadow of consumerism, abusive depletion of irreplaceable natural resources and generation of pollution on a shocking global scale.

At the same time, social inequity has increased beyond what is acceptable, safe and decent. The polarisations of wealth and obscene consumption have created disturbing inequities, which cause on the same day tonnes of food to be discarded, whilst the children of the same rich and wasteful cities go to school without breakfast. The fashion industry, which is the second greatest polluter after oil and gas, continues to churn out new and trendy garments, for quick disposable use, every six weeks, whilst global corporations cause ethical and ecological outrage on the one hand whilst at the same time washing the other with so-called corporate responsibility gestures that see large amounts of money donated to charities as a tax-deductible mechanism. The difference in pay between average employees in organisations and the CEOs of the same organisations can now be as much as 250 times. Business leadership is rewarded for short-term gains and long-term failure, whilst politicians have utterly lost respect and meaning of their roles and ruthlessly pursue selfish personal interests.

Something is seriously wrong with this picture, and the younger generations are increasingly concerned and vocal about the type of legacy that is being handed over to them. It is a legacy of eroded ethical principles, a planet traumatised by ecological neglect and a social fabric where social mobility and work opportunities for individuals to fulfil potential have been severely curtailed by divisions between those who have and those who have not.

The tensions exists everywhere on the planet and manifest through the usual perverted mechanisms of scapegoating, marginalisation, acts of violence and terror, political instability and financial volatility, all on the backdrop of a fragile ecosystem which has been relentlessly plundered for decades.

The awareness of complexity, volatility and unpredictability of the future is increasing, and the rise of artificial intelligence (AI), which has tremendously supported automation but appears now to be set to further replace human contributions in the workplace, has also given rise to a completely new definition of work, skills, professions and business models.

Business as usual can no longer be conducted, and the latest mantra is that because the future is unpredictable and unknown, we are somewhat powerless to intervene or demonstrate leadership and will in the direction and decisions that business owners and leaders can make.

But whilst it is true that we can never quite predict the future, it is also true that our anxiety and disempowerment are not entirely justified.

We have accumulated a vast body of scientific and experiential knowledge, the amount of published and literally available at our fingertips is vast and the list of domains of knowledge which can be effectively applied in business is really long.

What seems to be lacking is not the access to the know how to manage and control the system but lack of clarity and intent on which direction to position business decisions.

Clarity on this higher level of thinking about business direction sits with defining purpose, mission and vision and making sure they absolutely connect to service and benefits for the wider society and the planet, with a focus to redress the disrupted equilibrium and reverse the harm already done.

Common sense alone should be enough to inform us on what is right and what is wrong, whilst knowledge and experience can give us the methods and the how to implement such a strategy if we care to choose this path.

For small, medium and large organisations, the size is an advantage, even more so for businesses that are just started up or are at a point of growth and transformation. This is the opportunity for all those connected to business, to re-define and re-design not only the output of a business but also, more important, what it stands for.

This type of thinking and aspirations inform the SOCIETAL-ByDesign™ Model, positioned to facilitate transformation and implementation for those who choose to think about business beyond profit, at times when business activity and processes are in train and will undoubtedly impact not only employees but society and planet at large. The model introduces purpose, principles, metrics, a framework and dynamic mechanisms of transformation, which can be useful as a guide or standard for individual enterprises to adopt and adapt.

The SOCIETALByDesign™ Model can also be seen as a controlled correction mechanism whereby we are empowered to choose and chart our future rather than allow consumerism, profit, technology, AI, corporations and the stock exchange to inflict "corrections" on us – such as the financial crash of 2009, for example – in ways that we may not like and leave no choices for those left still standing but to mop up after being hit by a technological, financial or ecological tsunami.

Millennials and the generations after them are increasingly aware and demanding of urgent change in current and future business practices. Society is restless and unhappy with the position we now find ourselves and is using increasingly direct actions to signal impatience.

The fact is that whilst we may never be able to quite predict the future with full accuracy, we can certainly predict a long list of controllable causality, which allows us a strong hand on the steering – based on the cultural accumulation of our human civilisation, the collective wisdom and the specific scientific and business practice knowledge – for a forthcoming journey in which at least half of it is known and under our control.

Let us not squander the tremendous value of the vast amount of things that we know and give in to the excuse of helpless submission to the unknown.

We know about the laws of biology, society and business just as we know about gravity. And it is respecting an understanding gravity that enables our space programs to go to the edge of our universe and build glass and steel towers soaring towards the sky.

Our existing knowledge enables us, and we can control at least half of our social, business, economic and political fate. Let us use our power for what is good for society and nature. Making the right choices for business, people and the planet are not about political or religious colours. It is about policy, wisdom, will and respect of humanity and the continuity of our human civilisation.

WE CAN go FAR if we are SOCIETAL and EMPOWER ourselves. Let us set our sights far and high, with hope and confidence, onto a future that hold the unknown, including tremendous possibilities for healing and prosperity for all, if only we choose to navigate the space and time in between, repairing, restoring, nurturing and respecting rather than plundering and devouring.

Human existence has a 40,000 years of history proving how ingenuity and superior creativity combined with higher cognition and need for meaning and purpose have enabled our existence and progress. Let us make good and constructive use of this significant heritage of wisdom and cultural accumulation and be remembered for our own constructive contributions and positive legacy that enhance the life and civilisation of our planet!

Bibliography

Csíkszentmihályi, M. (2003). *Good business: Leadership, flow, and the making of meaning.* New York: Penguin Books.

Tarry, A. (2018). Coaching and technology: Revolution or co-evolution? *Coaching at Work*, 13(5), Sept.–Oct., pp. 40–43.

Tarry, A. (2018). The fourth revolution: Ethics and technology must shake hands. But can they, and what has this got to do with coaches? *Coaching at Work*, 13(4), July–Aug., pp. 39–41.

Torbert, B. (2004). *Action inquiry: The secret of timely and transforming leadership.* San Francisco, CA: Berrett-Koehler.

Index